# FAMILY THERAPY

# BASICS

# FAMILY THERAPY
# BASICS

**Mark Worden**
*Fairfield University*

**Brooks/Cole Publishing Company**
Pacific Grove, California

The trademark ITP is used under license.

 A CLAIREMONT BOOK

**Brooks/Cole Publishing Company**
A Division of Wadsworth, Inc.

Printed in the United States of America

10  9  8  7  6  5  4  3  2  1

**Library of Congress Cataloging-in-Publication Data**

Worden, Mark, [date]
    Family therapy basics / Mark Worden.
        p.    cm.
    Includes bibliographical references and index.
    ISBN 0-534-23076-8
    1. Family psychotherapy.    I. Title.
    RC488.5.W67    1993
    616.89'156—dc20                          93-29240
                                                 CIP

Sponsoring Editor:   *Claire Verduin*
Editorial Associate:   *Gay C. Bond*
Production Editor:   *Marjorie Z. Sanders*
Manuscript Editor:   *Bill Waller*
Permissions Editor:   *Elaine Jones*
Interior and Cover Design:   *Michael Rogondino*
Art Coordinator and Interior Illustration:   *Lisa Torri*
Typesetting:   *Kachina Typesetting, Inc.*
Printing and Binding:   *Malloy Lithographing, Inc.*

*To all the families who have
taught me my craft*

# Contents

# Preface

"The theories make sense to me, but what do I do for an entire session with a live family?" lamented a beginning therapist facing his first family session. That statement, first uttered to me in supervision, captured the dilemma and anxiety of the beginning family therapist. About to complete a master's degree, the trainee was well versed in a variety of theories of family therapy. He could distinguish strategic from structural approaches. He was facile in discussing differentiation and triangles. Family boundaries and coalitions made exquisite sense to him. But he had been awed at workshops where wizard-like masters made magical leaps of intuition, and he doubted whether he could ever do the same. And now, faced with his first interview, he felt a great gap between what he had learned in textbooks and what he was actually going to do in this upcoming session.

Paying closer attention to the questions that supervisees were asking, I felt many of them could be summarized by a simple question, "What do I do next?" This is not a request for a conceptual discussion but a very pragmatic, down-to-earth, action-oriented question. Time after time it occurred to me that beginning family therapists—and even though my memory fades, I still remember my own terror in my first few sessions—experience great difficulty translating theories into action and, consequently, lack a good map that would help them navigate the choppy waters of a family therapy session.

This book, therefore, addresses the needs of the beginning clinician by providing a process, or "nuts-and-bolts," introduction to family therapy—a reference book, if you will, for actually conducting family interviews. A thorough discussion of theoretical models, however, is left to other texts as a professor or supervisor deems appropriate. Instead, the book provides the student or trainee with practical guidelines for conducting family interviews (and, it's hoped, relieves much of the anxiety of actually working with families), emphasizes common clinical problems, and serves as a springboard for theoretical and clinical discussions. To aid the reader, conceptual terms are boldfaced in the text and are defined in glossaries at the end of chapters.

To accomplish its purpose, the book divides the treatment process into phases: the first interview, engagement, the middle phase, and termination.

The chapter contents include steps in conducting a first interview, establishing therapeutic boundaries and the therapist's use of self, the identification of family dysfunctional patterns, a discussion of the models for change and the role of resistance in change, techniques in promoting change, and termination within a developmental perspective.

Most chapters are divided into a conceptual discussion of a particular aspect or phase of treatment, the case presentation, and treatment notes. The treatment notes represent the therapist's internal dialogue: "Should I push for all family members to attend the next session?" "Should I let the father continue to dominate the session?" "How do I engage the adolescent?" And so forth. These notes pose therapeutic questions but also offer practical "here-and-now" answers.

Finally, a single family—Donna and Peter Martin, his teenage daughter from a previous marriage, and her two children—is followed through the entire treatment process. As a result, the case presentation provides a continuing focus for the discussion of clinical problems and their solutions. The text further emphasizes the therapeutic choice points that occur during a therapy session. In so doing, it strikes a balance between providing the reader with a conceptual understanding of the family treatment process and offering a variety of potential therapeutic interventions.

I am grateful to the reviewers, who have offered helpful suggestions: Maryanna Ham, University of Massachusetts at Boston; Susan Hendrick, Texas Tech University; Victoria A. McGillin, Wheaton College; Thomas Millard, Montclair State College; and Elizabeth A. Sirles, University of Wisconsin at Milwaukee. A special thanks to the staff of Brooks/Cole and, in particular, Claire Verduin for her encouragement and Bill Waller for his thoughtful editing.

*Mark Worden*

# FAMILY THERAPY
# BASICS

# 1

# The Movement to Systems

*Individual versus systems dynamics*
*Lineal versus circular causality*
*Content versus process*
*Summary*
*Overview of the book*

"You're lying!" yells 16-year-old Randy.

"No, I'm not, and don't talk to me in that tone!" strikes back his father, Mr. James.

A sneer forms on Randy's face, while Mr. James glares threateningly at his son.

Meanwhile, Mrs. James sits anxiously fearing an escalation; Randy's 11-year-old sister, Susan, nervously shifts in her chair; next to Mrs. James sits 8-year-old Alice, sucking her thumb.

At this point the battle lines are drawn, the spectators are seated, and the moment freezes for what seems an interminable time. As the room fills with raw hostility, a thought passes through the therapist's mind: "Is it too late to see them each individually or refer them individually to other therapists? In fact, why don't I suggest individual sessions with the son? That will certainly take the tension out of the room, and besides, that's what the parents came in for anyway: to fix their son!"

In retrospect, family therapy looked more fulfilling and less problematic to the therapist in the textbooks.

This reaction is common when one begins to work with families. In contrast to individual psychotherapy, where the therapist-client dyad is much more predictable, therapist-family interactions may occur at a fast and furious pace, at times seemingly running out of control. At other times the family exchanges may be guarded, suspicious, and infrequent, with each member unwilling to volunteer any information and silence dominating the session. Nevertheless, what becomes clear to a beginning family therapist is that the more family members are added to the room (an increase in individual dynamics), the more the clinical data multiply.

In the case of the James family, the father-son conflict would occur at the drop of a hat and possessed the power to rivet everyone's attention. Seemingly, any topic mentioned would quickly evoke a father-son face-off and demand the therapist's attention. In reaction to the emotional power of the arguments and the wealth of clinical data in the room, beginning family therapists are most likely to find themselves falling back on familiar turf. This is accomplished by narrowing the clinical focus back to the individual dynamics: What is the son's fury all about? Why does the father need control over such trivial matters? And so forth.

Likewise, questions of causality and change swirl in the therapist's head. For example, the family would function better if the father were less controlling or if the son could only break from his fear of dependency and quit confronting his father. With this in mind, the therapist would begin to focus on changing one or both individuals. Or, as is more often the case, the therapist would attempt to negotiate a settlement between the two parties.

Unfortunately, each session bears a striking resemblance to the previous one: A topic is brought up, the son complains, the father argues back, and the downward spiral of conflict erupts. Caught in this cycle of futility, the therapist frequently applies more of the same by trying to get the father to be less controlling and the son to accept some of the father's limits. To accomplish this, the therapist solicits a compromise:

**Therapist:**   Now Mr. James, if you would just allow a later curfew and if your son would just abide by these reasonable limits, there might be less fighting going on.

What the therapist soon discovers, however, is that what appears to be a reasonable intervention in the office—at least the father and son are sitting silently at the end of the session—dissolves within a week when one or both parties violate the agreement and the circular battles in the therapy sessions erupt again. At this point the therapist is faced with a nagging question: "Now what do I do? The father will not back down from trying to control his son, and the son appears compelled to continually confront the father's rules."

To answer the "now what" question, the therapist, rather than trying to change individual behavior, shifts perspective or epistemology and focuses on the family system. In so doing, the therapist moves to another level of conceptualization. Specifically, this epistemological shift occurs on three key dimensions:

1. a movement from individual to systems dynamics
2. a circular versus a lineal view of causality
3. content versus process dynamics

# Individual versus Systems Dynamics

The power and pull of focusing on individual dynamics in therapy are reinforced by the wealth and depth of existing individual personality theories, the findings of developmental psychology concentrating on the individual, individually oriented psychiatric diagnostic categories, and one's personal idiosyncratic experiences.

Beginning first and foremost with Freudian, intrapsychic, psychodynamic theory, you have probably been exposed to a variety of personality theories in any number of undergraduate and graduate courses. The theories center on the individual's experience on both the conscious and unconscious levels: intrapersonal experiences. Likewise, developmental psychology courses address the stages of individual development. True, some attention is paid to the interaction with others (social development), but the centerpiece is the individual responding to internal demands. In addition, current psychiatric diagnostic categories, based on the medical model, demand an individual perspective. Disorders exist and reside within the person. And finally, we are all most familiar with our own phenomenological experience in the world. Individual perspective is certainly a valid commodity, because we all have it all the time.

But what, then, is this family systems viewpoint all about? What does it add to our conceptualization of clinical problems and our desire to help our clients?

Briefly, by moving to the next level of analysis—from the individual system to the family system—we see a family not merely as a collection of individuals but as a whole that is greater than the sum of its parts. Consequently, individual behavior is understood within the context of the whole, and the family becomes an entity of analysis in and of itself—an entity that seeks stability (**morphostasis** or **homeostasis**) in the face of environmental vagaries but at other times must change its structure (**morphogenesis**) to better adapt to internal and external demands. In other words, just as we can perceive a person as a developing entity responding to both internal and external forces and also seeking a sense of stability and continuity, we can observe the family in a similar fashion.

More to the point, a systems perspective offers a means of conceptualizing the wealth of data gathered in a family session as well as providing a foundation to plan and implement interventions. Individual behavior, therefore, no longer occurs in isolation but is embedded within the broader family context. Consequently, an individual family member's problematic or symptomatic behavior is seen as an outcome of family interactions and not a result of individual dynamics. In other words, from a systems perspective the therapist distinguishes between the forest (family dynamics) and the trees (individual dynamics).

Rather than staying on the conceptual plane, however, we can apply systems concepts to the James family.

Sixteen-year-old Randy was referred by his school psychologist for failing grades and unexcused absences. He was judged as "highly at risk" by school personnel. Both parents readily agreed to counseling because they had increasingly felt that Randy's behavior was beyond their control. The family, as we have seen, consisted of Mr. James (43 years of age), Mrs. James (42), Randy (16), Susan (11), and Alice (8).

From all accounts, there were few problems in the family until Randy began high school. Mr. and Mrs. James felt that he then began to pull away from the family and continually test his parents' authority: arguments began over clothes, friends, curfew, and the like. From Randy's perspective, all he wanted was "a little freedom" to make his own decisions.

Simplified, the family pattern was for Randy to violate one of his parents' rules. His father would then confront him, leading to an argument that would quickly escalate into a screaming match between the two. At that point Mrs. James would enter the skirmish in an attempt to "calm them down before someone got hurt." More often than not, she would pull Randy away from his father and attempt to soothe her son. As for the two younger sisters, Susan would be in her room but listening to every angry word, while Alice would seek her mother out in order to nurture and be nurtured.

From a systems perspective, the emergence of adolescence in one or more of the children, particularly the oldest child, is **feedback** (a circular message) within a family that change is required. Specifically, a transformation needs to occur within the parent-child relationship that permits greater autonomy for the blossoming young adult while still maintaining a sense of belonging among the family members (Worden, 1991). In the James family, the **rules** (overtly or covertly agreed-to relationship patterns that organize the system) guiding the parent-child relationship established when the children were younger were ill-suited for a parent-adolescent relationship. Concretely, the means of disciplining and guiding an 8-year-old are different from the parental practices effective with a 16-year-old. The James family, moreover, was experiencing great difficulty changing or transforming (morphogenesis) the parent-child relationship into a parent-adolescent one. Mr. James's position was that a child was always a child as long as he or she continued to live under the family roof.

Moreover, within the family, both the rules and **roles** (individually prescribed patterns of behavior) were quite rigid. Children were to be seen and not heard, a rule Mr. James enforced with an iron hand. He was clearly the autocrat in the family and had a dogmatic idea of right and wrong; consequently, Randy's rebellious behavior was intolerable. Mr. James was the Judge and Sergeant-at-Arms attempting to bring order to his home. Mrs. James was the Peacekeeper. Randy was the Victim or Rebel, depending upon one's point of view. Susan was the Innocent Bystander caught in conflict she had no hand in creating or controlling. Alice was the Lost Child wanting to be nurtured.

The family's **boundaries** (emotional barriers that protect and enhance the integrity of individuals, subsystems, and families) were relatively impermeable to the outside environment: "I don't care what other kids are allowed to do; as long as you live under my roof you will follow my rules." But they were internally **diffuse.** That is, the family's **subsystem boundaries** were poorly defined. Family members were not permitted a sense of individuality, which was sacrificed for the greater whole. For example, Randy was not allowed to spend very much time alone in his room. What was normal adolescent developmental behavior, sitting in his room with the radio blasting, was viewed by the parents as a rejection of the family.

Clinically, when viewed from a systems perspective, Randy's "rebellious" behavior is placed within the family context, and thus the definition of the problem broadens. The question "What is wrong with Randy?" shifts to "What is the function, purpose, or meaning of Randy's behavior within the family dynamics?" For example, several initial systems hypotheses might be:

1. Randy's behavior reflects the family's inability to transform a parent-child relationship into a parent-adolescent one.
2. Randy's behavior is the steam valve on the family's boiling kettle; his blowups release built-up pressures—that is, marital problems.
3. Randy's behavior is an outgrowth of his parents' inability to set reasonable, consistent, and fair limits.
4. Randy and his father are fighting over Mrs. James's attention.
5. Randy is fighting his father in defense of what he perceives to be his mother's oppression by his father.

Furthermore, when viewed from a system's perspective, the level of intervention also shifts. Individual therapy with Randy is complemented or replaced with family therapy. Embedded in the family's interactional patterns, Randy's behavior changes as the family changes. Thus, modifying the **family system** (the family's structure or organization and its interactional patterns) becomes the focus of treatment.

## *Lineal versus Circular Causality*

Just as the movement to a systems model changes the definition of the problem, the shift in perspective also changes one's view of causality—from lineal to circular. With **lineal causality,** event A causes event B; the dominoes are in a straight line and fall in sequence. Applying this line of reasoning to the James family, the following would be hypothesized:

1. If Randy would only obey his parents and stop his rebellious behavior, everything would be fine in the family.
2. If Randy were only granted more freedom, his rebellious behavior would stop.
3. If Mr. James would stop being so intrusive with his son, Randy would be less angry and more likely to comply with his parents' wishes.
4. If the father-son relationship could be improved, Randy's behavior would change.
5. If Mrs. James would only consistently support her husband in his battles with their son, Randy would get a united message from his parents and obey.

It follows that choosing any of the above lines of reasoning will strongly determine the therapist's behavior. For example, if Randy's behavior is seen as the cause of the family's disruption, individual therapy is the treatment of choice. Even if family therapy is employed, the therapist's behavior may still be strongly influenced by the lineal assumptions. For instance, if the father is seen as the "cause" of Randy's behavior, changing Mr. James within the family session becomes the therapist's overt or covert agenda.

Circular causality, on the other hand, places individual behavior within a network of **circular feedback loops** (an individual family member's behavior affects other family members who in turn affect the individual). Thus, the cause and effect of lineal causality becomes purely arbitrary; an individual's behavior is in reaction to others but also influences others. For one to say, therefore, that one person causes another's behavior misses the point; rather, person A affects B and C as much as B and C affect A in reciprocal interactions.

Returning to the James family, Randy was reacting to his father's seemingly inappropriate restrictions, but Mr. James was restricting him because his son was so out of control. Mrs. James was trying to be fair to both her husband and son, but her behavior only served to make both of them angrier because she appeared to be supporting one against the other. In turn, both Randy and his father became increasingly angry at each other and at Mrs. James. Consequently, Mr. James had to prove to his wife how out of control Randy was, and Randy, in turn, had to show how unfair his father was. Finally, Susan vicariously absorbed the conflict and was potentially destined to act out herself, while the nurturing that Alice wanted was lost in the family battles. Thus, each member's behavior directly influences others' behavior, and shifts in one part of the system reverberate throughout the system.

Circular causality, therefore, draws the therapist's attention away from seeing individuals as causing behavior in others to a broader view of the family's repeating and self-perpetuating cycles of interaction. Cycles may be functional (adaptive for the family) or dysfunctional (maladaptive for the family by producing symptomatic behavior in one or more family members). Moreover, these repeating and self-perpetuating cycles of interaction weave the family's life tapestry. In terms of family psychotherapy, therefore, the family's dysfunctional patterns become the focus of assessment and intervention.

Finally, circular causality eliminates the "bad guy" assumption. As will be discussed in a later chapter, families typically present the explanations of their problems in lineal terms: If only he or she quit doing that, we would all live in peace. Such a definition of the problem frequently produces a **family scapegoat** (the family member who is blamed for the disruptions and tension). Depending upon the therapist's lineal perspective, for example, Randy might be the cause of the family's problems, or Mr. James could be the culprit.

Circular causality, however, argues that there is no "bad guy"—a family member who is entirely to blame for the problem—but, rather, that each member is mutually and reciprocally shaping the behavior of others and that what emerges from this reciprocal shaping are patterns that are discernible and may be more or less functional or dysfunctional for the family.

## Content versus Process

The shift to a systems model also raises the distinction between content and process, both in the presenting problem and in the therapy sessions. **Content** refers to the concrete issue being discussed in the session—the "what" that is being said—whereas process refers to how the issue is portrayed in the family's interactions. In other words, **process** is the systematic series of interactions that underlies the content discussion. For example, the James's arguments could be over any number of content issues: Randy's attitude, his choice of friends, his school performance, his curfew, and so forth. Nevertheless, the process of these arguments—the family's underlying, repetitive, dysfunctional problem-solving pattern—was the same regardless of which content issue was at center stage at any particular moment in therapy.

To further elaborate, Mr. and Mrs. James presented their problem as their son's behavior. When asked to specify their problem more clearly, they expressed a desire to change Randy (lineal causality). Initially, they brought up any number of problems with their son that they wanted changed: improved school performance, obeying their rules, a better attitude toward them, and so on. Notwithstanding, the therapist was concerned with the process issues:

- How does Randy's behavior fit into the family patterns?
- Why did Randy's behavior evolve at this time?

- How do the family members solve their problems?
- How does each shape and reinforce the others' behavior?
- What is the function of Randy's behavior in the family system?

Most importantly, the therapist was concerned with the last question. Papp (1983) points out that a current controversy in the family therapy field is whether the symptom (Randy's behavior) serves a homeostatic function (morphostasis—keeping the family the same) or an evolutionary function (morphogenesis—encouraging the system to evolve new patterns of functioning).

From a homeostatic line of reasoning, Randy may play a part in a covert marital conflict. That is to say, his acting-out behavior focuses the family's attention on him and thus distracts the parents from their own personal disagreements. Consequently, it is easier for the parents to argue over Randy than to face their disappointments in each other. Moreover, their marital conflicts do not surface to threaten the family's existence, and the tenuous balance in the family is maintained. From this vantage point, Randy is sacrificing himself to preserve the family unit.

Another homeostatic hypothesis is that Randy's behavior maintains the child orientation of the family. Adolescence signals a separation from parents and a movement to young adulthood. What may be a welcome relief to some parents is a threat to others, particularly in the area of control. If Randy remains a child, the family's homeostasis (on the control dimension) is maintained. For example, and ironically, Randy's acting-out behavior did not foster his independence but served to increase adults' control over his life as both school personnel and his parents placed increased limits on him. He protested that he wanted freedom but acted in ways that forced adults to impose greater restrictions on him. Thus, he was viewed by his parents not as a young, emerging adult but still as a child in need of control.

In contrast, the evolutionary line of reasoning (morphogenesis) would argue that Randy's behavior is pushing the family to a new level of organization. By rebelling and fighting against what he perceives as his family's restrictiveness—"They want me to be just like them"—Randy is forcing the family to reorganize itself and, therefore, grow. His behavior is screaming loud and clear that the family's homeostasis, although effective when all the children were below the age of 10, is inappropriate for a 16-year-old teenager/young adult. Adolescents' symptoms may signal a blocked developmental sequence, and a "better fit" between them and the family may need to evolve (Worden, 1991). Thus, from an evolutionary viewpoint, the family sitting in your office can be seen as an organization strained by new demands—internal or external pressures—but responding in old, ineffective patterns and thus increasing its "problems."

As you can see, the shift in attention from content—what the family presents as its problem—to process issues—the balance of morphostatic and morphogenetic forces in the family—is a dramatic one for the therapist. The content-oriented therapist would be busy with the James family attempting to resolve or negotiate each of the content issues: Randy's curfew, choice of friends, and school performance level. The process-oriented therapist, however, would be searching for the dysfunctional patterns that underlie the content complaints: What is blocking the family from solving its own problems? Or how or why are morphostatic forces dominating the James family?

## Summary

Individual models of behavior extend poorly to family dynamics. As the early pioneers in family therapy began breaking from their own theoretical pasts and started working with families, they saw a need to conceptualize the wealth of new data available as they added family members to the treatment process. Cybernetics and general systems theory offered the foundation to build a new treatment modality. This modality emphasized a systems perspective of behavior, circular causality, and process over content.

It must be stressed, however, that a systems paradigm in no way diminishes other established models. Much can be gained from a solid grasp of human developmental theory and individually oriented models, such as psychoanalysis, behaviorism, humanism, cognitive therapy, and so forth. In fact, a well-rounded clinician benefits from a knowledge of these areas.

Nevertheless, a systems perspective does offer a unique means of conceptualizing behavior as the clinician moves from an individual level of analysis to the family level. In the face of an emotional string of firecrackers going off in your office, you can use a systems perspective to order this cacophony and, equally important, develop intervention strategies that flow from this broader perspective.

Finally, as you will discover with further reading and the courses you will take, the term *systems theory* means different things to different people. Overall, it is a generic term for conceptualizing a group of related elements (family members) that interact as a whole entity (the family). Above anything else, it is more a way of thinking than a coherent, standardized theory (Nichols & Schwartz, 1991). Its strengths, nevertheless, are its ability to place an individual within the family context, drawing attention to how family members relate and thus opening new avenues to assessment and intervention.

## Overview of the Book

There are diverse models of family and systems therapy: psychoanalytic, transgenerational, group, symbolic-experiential, behavioral, contextual, Ericksonian, focal, psychoeducational, strategic, and structural (Gurman

& Kniskern, 1991). Each of these conceptual models offers its own unique perspective and assumptions of family functioning, symptom formation, and interventions. It is beyond the scope of this book to explore any of these in depth and to discuss their assumptions; besides, these tasks are accomplished much better in existing texts: Goldenberg & Goldenberg (1991), Gurman & Kniskern (1991), Nichols & Schwartz (1991), and Piercy & Sprenkle (1986). Instead, I hope to elaborate on the above themes of systems dynamics, circular causality, and a process orientation to provide a pragmatic overview of the basics of family psychotherapy. The topics and concepts that are sampled cover a broad range of family therapy approaches. They were selected because of their universality and familiarity to most family therapists. Despite an attempt to balance a variety of approaches for the beginning family therapist, the text reflects my own bias toward structural and strategic models. This is most evident in the assessment of dysfunctional family patterns and the preference for making those patterns the focus of treatment, particularly in the "here and now" of the therapy session.

Each chapter is divided into an initial conceptual discussion intertwined with case material and treatment notes. Although this is not quite a how-to book, the following chapters are intended to demonstrate the challenge of working with families and to increase your comfort in conducting family therapy.

Chapter 2, for example, outlines the steps in the initial phase of treatment: the first interview. Case content is contrasted with process observations that the therapist may make in assessing family patterns and building a therapeutic alliance. The chapter also introduces the Martin family, which will be followed throughout the different phases of treatment. (To protect confidentiality, the case is an amalgamation of families I have worked with in therapy.) By following one case, you should be able to capture the full flavor of working with a family from initial interview through termination.

Chapter 3 examines the therapeutic alliance developed in the initial phase of treatment. It pays particular attention to the role of the therapist in engaging family members in the process of therapy. And it argues that therapeutic possibilities increase when a strong alliance is forged.

Because family patterns are intricately tied to a systems approach, Chapter 4 offers a conceptual, but practical, introduction to assessing patterns of behavior. Concretely, the chapter gives examples of questions the therapist can ask to further delineate family patterns.

After the therapist has identified family patterns and established a working alliance with the members, the middle phase of treatment is concerned with implementing change. Chapter 5 discusses the therapist's and family's Dance of Change within their sessions. In particular, the therapist's ability to challenge family norms without overloading the members' anxiety is emphasized. Also, attempts at change are frequently met with resistance; consequently, identifying and responding to treatment impasses are keys to therapeutic success.

Specific interventions and techniques are discussed in Chapter 6. In designing and implementing interventions, the therapist is matching the appropriate technique with the family system at a time in treatment that captures the opportunities for change. Five types of intervention are discussed: process, structural, historical, paradoxical, and homework.

Chapter 7 discusses the final phase of treatment, termination. The guidelines for termination include assessing whether goals have been reached, identifying potential problems, and leaving the door open for future contacts.

# *Glossary*

**Boundaries**   Emotional barriers that protect and enhance the integrity of individuals, subsystems, and families; also, rules defining patterns of interaction; types of boundaries are: **Enmeshed**—overly weak, or **diffuse,** boundaries that poorly delineate the system's subsystems. **Disengaged**—overly strong boundaries that rigidly divide the system's subsystems. **Subsystem**—boundaries between smaller units embedded within a larger system; a subsystem may include individuals, siblings, parents, and members of the extended family.

**Circular causality**   A sequence of cause and effect whereby the explanation for a pattern leads back to the first cause and either confirms or changes that first cause; A causes B causes C that causes or modifies A.

**Circular feedback loops**   The process by which an individual family member's behavior affects other members, who in turn affect the individual.

**Content**   The concrete issues being discussed in a therapy session.

**Family scapegoat**   A family member on whom the family's difficulties and emotional upheaval are blamed.

**Family system**   The family's structure or organization and the members' interactive patterns.

**Feedback**   A circular message within a system.

**Homeostasis**   A system's tendency toward stability, or steady state.

**Lineal causality**   A cause-and-effect relationship such that the sequence does not come back to the starting point: A causes B causes C causes D and so on.

**Morphogenesis**   The formation and development of structures in a system; delineates the system-enhancing behavior that allows for growth, creativity, innovation, and other change.

**Morphostasis**   The ability of a system to maintain its structure in a changing environment; similar to homeostasis.

**Process** Interpersonal dynamics and interactional patterns underlying content issues.

**Roles** Individually prescribed patterns of behavior reinforced by the expectations and norms of the family.

**Rules** Overt or covert agreements within a family that organize the members' interaction into a reasonably stable system.

# 2

# The First Interview: Initiating Assessment and Engagement

**Developing the capacity to observe**
**Basic interactive concepts**
**The first interview**
**Summary**

The first interview begins two crucial processes for therapeutic success: engagement and assessment. Engagement, on the one hand, involves the forming of a therapeutic alliance between the therapist and family, a trusting alliance that permits them to explore the inner workings of family relationships. (The engagement process is introduced in this chapter, and a more detailed discussion follows in the next chapter.) Assessment, on the other hand, is the process of identifying the family's interactional patterns and, in particular, focusing on those patterns directly related to the problem behavior. After a first interview, the therapist has ideally begun to formulate working hypotheses about family patterns that are producing and maintaining the symptomatic behavior.

In traditional psychiatric models, diagnosing a person is a two-step process. First, an assessment of the client's internal experience, via self-report, and observations of the person's behavior are made. Second, these data are placed into categories and given a label, which serves as a shorthand means of summarizing the individual's symptoms. The movement to a family systems perspective, however, radically changes the concept of assessment and diagnosis.

First and foremost, one family member is not being singled out as possessing a disorder. Rather, the family becomes the unit of analysis. The data the therapist gathers consist of intrapersonal experiences—how each family member thinks and feels about the problem, particularly his or her view of others' behavior and motivations—and observable interactional patterns that occur in the sessions. Obviously, the more family members are added to this assessment, the greater the wealth of clinical material at the therapist's disposal. The question, therefore, is how to organize this material in a meaningful way that will also guide the therapeutic process.

As a guide for the therapist, specific diagnosis/assessment schemata grow directly out of the various theories of family therapy (Liddle, 1983). For example, a symbolic-experiential family therapist would assess, among other dimensions, the family members' ability to tolerate interpersonal stress and to play with one another, whereas a strategic therapist would view the symptoms as metaphors for adaptation in the family.

Based on a comparison of six schools (Bowen, symbolic-experiential, structural, strategic, brief, and systemic), Liddle (1983) concludes that although many differences exist, all the models share an appreciation for the need to understand family rules (cyclical behavioral patterns). Also, all the models link the rigidity of roles and patterns of interaction to dysfunction.

Thus, all family therapists, to one degree or another, concern themselves with rigid patterns or cycles that accompany any problem (Hoffman, 1981; Minuchin & Fishman, 1981). Consequently, one of the most challenging aspects of the movement to systems thinking, and one of the most difficult for beginning therapists, is developing the capacity to discern family interactional patterns as they evolve in the treatment sessions.

## *Developing the Capacity to Observe*

The skill in identifying family patterns lies first and foremost in the therapist's capacity to observe. Frequently, individually trained clinicians are reluctant to meet with families because of the wealth and even overload of data generated in family interviews. It is much clearer to meet with individuals and focus on their intrapersonal dynamics. More to the point, the dyadic nature of individual therapy allows for a much more controlled pace. There are no tempers flaring, people interrupting one another, or angry stares flashing across the room that may mark a family session. Moreover, attempting to understand the individual dynamics of four, five, six, or more people at the same time is simply overwhelming. Thus, discerning patterns becomes the first step in making sense out of a family session.

A key to discerning patterns is observing the verbal and nonverbal communication between family members. For example, and employing a form of shorthand:

- Where do people sit in relationship to one another?
- Who speaks for the family and may also speak for other members?
- How does the spokesperson introduce the family's problems?
- How do other family members react to the spokesperson's presentation? Does anyone object or agree?
- Who supports whom most frequently during the discussion?

- Which relationships are most conflictual?
- What are the common patterns to the family's disagreements?
- Who gets involved in these arguments? Who stays out of them?
- At what points are the therapist invited into the disagreements?
- Who consistently elicits the therapist's support?

With these and other similar questions in mind, the therapist is simultaneously listening to the family's concerns but also observing its consistent patterns. Basic patterns frequently emerge as soon as the therapist asks what the problem is and reemerge several times in the first interview. The content of the conflict may vary, but the patterns consistently reappear. A mother complains about her daughter, for example, the daughter counters her mother, anger escalates, the mother invites the father into the battle but he declines, he abdicates and looks to the therapist to solve the problem, and the mother feels increasingly frustrated and unsupported, which only furthers the argument with her daughter.

The next section introduces several basic concepts as a means of identifying patterns. In keeping with the tenor of the book, the list borrows from various family therapy theories, but the terms are familiar to most family therapists.

# Basic Interactive Concepts

## Triangulation and Scapegoating

Bowen (1978) maintains that a dyad (mother-father) is an unstable relationship system that forms a triangle (mother-father-child) under stress. Hoffman (1981) adds that triadic relationships are at the heart of family systems therapy.

"Triangling" a third party into a dyadic conflict is a common pattern for all of us. In a conflict between two friends, each will turn to a third friend to get his or her point of view. In a disagreement between a parent and child, the parent turns to the other parent for support, and the child turns to a friend or sibling for support: "Let me tell you what she did then!"

Accepting that **triangulation** is a reoccurring pattern in human relationships, when does it become dysfunctional? Hoffman (1981) speaks of the pressure on a child when each parent attempts to enlist the child's support against the other parent. In this scenario, the child is inappropriately elevated into the marital conflict and, under this stress, develops symptoms.

Covert marital conflict may also be managed by triangling in a child. In these cases, the child's symptoms dominate the family as the parents argue over which of them is to blame for the child's behavior. This allows the repressed marital anger to be displaced into the parents-child triangle. Ironi-

cally, this pattern protects the family's existence because the marital conflict that could lead toward separation or divorce remains hidden or unaddressed, and the parents may then express their anger toward each other as
parents, not as spouses, or toward the child. The overt conflicts concerning
the child serve as a steam valve for the boiling family tensions.

Marital conflict chronically managed by triangling in a child is dysfunctional on several levels. First, the marital conflict is never fully addressed, which continues to leave the "lump underneath the carpet."
Second, the child is inundated with stress messages that he or she can do
little about. Third, the child is, at best, torn by loyalty to each parent and, at
worse, subtly asked to choose one side against the other. And finally, the
family avoids developing more effective problem-solving skills.

A variation of the theme is when a scapegoat has been selected by the
family. In these cases, the pain caused by the dysfunctional triangles is
projected onto one of the family members (frequently one of the children):
"We would be happy if it weren't for you." Consequently, all stress, frustration, and anger are directed toward this family member. Tragically, with
time, this member will absorb the accusations and fulfill the family's
prophecy: "They don't think I can do anything right anyway, so I don't care
either!"

Interviewing these families may leave the therapist with a headache. It
is clear that there is a tremendous amount of anger in the room, but all of it
is being directed at one family member. Any attempts to move the discussion to other problems in the family or between other family members is
met with denial. One piece of evidence after another is exhibited to prove
the parents' point: "He did this. He did that. He doesn't listen. He won't
obey. He's out of control." In addition, the family has come in only to drop
off the scapegoat to be fixed: "Why do we all have to come? He's the
problem. Shouldn't you be seeing him alone?"

A more seductive form of scapegoating occurs when parents present
themselves as victims. In these cases the scapegoating has been going on for
so long that the child, most often now an adolescent, is a terror. The parents
look pleadingly at the therapist while their adolescent son, with a disdainful
look, is flicking matches into the corner. These scenes call out for the
therapist to do something with this teenager and, in the process, join
(triangle) with the parents.

## Boundaries

The structural theory of Salvador Minuchin (1974) places a heavy emphasis
on boundaries delineating the family's structure. As we saw in Chapter 1,
boundaries are unwritten rules that define the family interactions: who
participates and how. For example, can a child express anger at a parent?
Can a parent form a coalition with a child against the other parent? Can a

grandfather correct a grandchild when the father is in the room? Does the husband always put his mother's needs above his wife's needs? And so forth.

Boundaries serve to protect the differentiation of the family system (Minuchin, 1974). In a family structure that is clearly defined, the grandparents serve as an extended support subsystem for the nuclear family (parents and children). The parental subsystem makes the executive decisions for the family and permits the parents to mutually support each other while the children are free to interact with one another in learning the values of competition and cooperation.

Although they are not elaborated by Minuchin, one can also conceptualize interpersonal boundaries around each individual family member. The boundaries permit the "space" needed for personal growth. With clear individual boundaries, for instance, one's thoughts and feelings are respected; a person is not confined to a limited, acceptable range of behavior rigidly reinforced by family rules. Instead, differences are accepted in a family as a natural consequence of the members' unique personalities. This is particularly important in families with adolescents, because appropriate and clear interpersonal boundaries permit the teenager to individuate but at the same time remain connected to the family (Worden, 1991).

To return to the structural framework, boundaries (or transactional patterns) range on a dimension from enmeshed to disengaged. *Enmeshed* patterns blur boundaries. These families lack any clear demarcations of generational hierarchy (grandparents-parents-children). In turn, any sense of autonomy is sacrificed to the cost of belonging. Responding to family needs comes first, before individual desires or wants. A narrow range of acceptable behavior (thoughts, feelings, and actions) is permitted—the cost of belonging—and is reinforced through guilt. Telling people what they *should* think and feel is permissible. Deviance threatens the system's unity and, consequently, will be labeled "mad" or "bad" behavior. Thus, individual growth is greatly restricted.

In therapy, enmeshed boundaries are characterized by:

1. members speaking for one another
2. parents telling children what the children really think and feel or telling them what they should think and feel
3. guilt used as a means of controlling others
4. hints that neither parent has psychologically separated from his or her own parents

For example, in the course of ongoing treatment, a boy 9 years of age whose depressive symptoms had led the family to seek therapy said, "I'm lonely." Quickly, the family was energized, and the mother said: "You are *not* lonely. You have your grandparents, your parents, and your brother and sister." The father concurred and observed: "That's the silliest thing I ever heard. What's wrong with you to say such a thing?" In these interactions, the boy was being taught that his thoughts or feelings were not valid unless they concurred with the family norms. Furthermore, the boy was being clearly told that loneliness was not permitted in the family or, at the very least, that he had better not verbalize those feelings.

In contrast, *disengaged* boundaries sacrifice belonging for autonomy. Overly rigid or impermeable boundaries among people inhibit communication and rob the family of much-needed mutual support. Privacy is taken to the extreme. Little sharing of thoughts and feelings occurs, and family members typically seek support outside of the family in friends, activities, alcohol, and other drugs.

Families with disengaged boundaries are extremely reluctant to be in family therapy. It is too threatening. The members have operated by staying away from one another, and now this therapist wants to bring them together. As a result, the engagement phase of treatment is marked by the continuing efforts to persuade the therapist to meet individually with the scapegoat.

More specifically, it is sometimes erroneous to label a family as purely enmeshed or disengaged. More often than not, close examination of interpersonal boundaries among individual family members reveals a potpourri: son is enmeshed with mother but disengaged from father; father is disengaged from his own father but enmeshed with his daughter; parents are disengaged from one another, but each is enmeshed with one of the children.

In summary, enmeshed and disengaged boundaries inhibit effective problem solving in families and hamper individual members' growth. At either extreme the patterns are dysfunctional, because the members are unable to balance their strivings for autonomy and their need to belong.

## Power

Akin to the concept of a generational hierarchy (clear boundaries among grandparents, parents, and children) is the definition of power in a family: what members have the power in the family, how they got it, how they maintain it, and at what costs to other members. For the purpose of the following discussion, and defined simply, **power** is the ability to influence others.

Each family member has individual wants and needs. Sometimes through individual action members can satisfy their needs, but more often than not, family membership implies the cooperation and consideration of others if the majority of needs are to be met. Likewise, diverse individual needs may conflict, leading to frustration, hurt, and disappointment. A teenager cries for more freedom while the parents enforce restraint. A husband attempts to influence his wife while she attempts to influence him. Understanding these patterns, however, is frequently a difficult task because there is typically more there than meets the eye.

For example, a dominant, authoritarian father may initially appear to possess the power in the family. His wife and children behave in ways to avoid his anger. But on closer examination, the power is akin to shifting sands. The teenage son has the power to rebel and not follow orders. The father is powerless to change his son's rebellious behavior no matter how much he threatens. The mother, furthermore, has the power to further her son's rebellion against his father by silently encouraging her son.

What one sees when looking closely at family patterns is the way in which attempts to wield power are frequently countered by others, almost in an attempt to balance the power in the family. To continue with the above example, the mother has the power, by gathering the children around her, to exclude the father from the family's nurturing emotional life. The father, sensing his emotional exclusion but putting it in control words, accuses the mother of undercutting him: "You baby and protect that boy too much." For his part, the son allies with his mother because she gives him the freedom he wants when his father is not around. Thus, while a therapist may be quickly drawn into viewing the authoritarian father as the only one possessing power in the family, closer examination reveals power (again, the ability to influence) being expressed by each family member.

Power, therefore, has both overt and covert qualities. What initially appears to be the power hierarchy in the family shifts as the family patterns emerge. To avoid being bogged down in the overt, and typically obvious, power patterns in the family, the therapist asks three simple questions:

1. In what way is each family member attempting to influence others?
2. How is the overt power in the family counterbalanced by covert power?
3. How is each family member attempting to influence me [the therapist], particularly if someone is presenting himself or herself as the victim?

## Intimacy

It is erroneous to believe that there is one absolute way in which family members should express their closeness with one another. Members of some families are constantly touching one another both physically—a touch on the shoulder—and verbally—"I really do care about you." Others may sit stiffly, arms tightly at their sides, while another member cries. To judge as "good" or "bad" either of these styles or patterns misses the point: Each family has evolved its own unique ways of expressing affection and thus sharing closeness.

Appreciating the family's style of **intimacy** (the ability to form caring, expressive bonds while respecting individual boundaries) serves to guide the therapist during the engagement and intervention phases of therapy. For example, forcing people to spend time together or to share intimate thoughts may be ill-timed and may promote unnecessary anxiety and resistance. Likewise, attempting to create distance in an enmeshed relationship may also stir anxiety and create unnecessary resistance.

Again, three simple questions can guide the clinician:

1. How is intimacy expressed in this family (that is, are the family members comfortable with touching one another, sharing compliments, saying "I love you")?
2. Is there too little or too much intimacy for the members' needs?
3. How does the family's expression of intimacy differ from my own? Will this be a problem in my working with it?

## Communication Patterns

Although certainly an overused word, *communication* is at the heart of family patterns. Rather than attempting to elaborate on the variety of communication patterns and to avoid a redundancy of the previous discussion, I offer the following guidelines intended to improve your observational skills.

Verbal behavior:

- Who speaks to whom in the family?
- Do family members speak for one another?
- How often do sentences begin with *you* instead of *I*?
- Who tends to dominate the discussion?
- Does anyone try to interrupt that person?
- What types of words frequently occur in the discussion—that is, judgmental and evaluative words *(stupid, bad, good, foolish)*—or supportive words *(love, care, understand)*?
- What tones dominate the discussion—for example, hostility, pleading, anger, hurt, confusion?
- Do family members listen, or do they continually interrupt?

Nonverbal behavior (frequently more revealing than verbal):

- Do family members acknowledge one another when someone is talking—a nod of the head, eye contact?
- Who acknowledges whom, and who nonverbally avoids whom?
- Where do members consistently sit in relation to one another?
- Who leads the family into the office?
- When members speak, do they continually look at the therapist and not the person about whom they are speaking?
- Is physical contact made among family members?
- What is the quality of that contact—comforting or forced and stiff?

Although more guidelines could be added, the point is that the verbal and nonverbal interactions between family members are grist for the family therapist's mill. Developing the ability to listen to the speaker while simultaneously observing other family members is a key therapeutic skill. Furthermore, your skill is enhanced by being able to follow the action and reaction of the communication patterns: How does a family member react when he or she is accused? How does this response fuel further exchanges and potentially triangle in other family members or the therapist?

# The First Interview

In the initial session, many therapeutic agendas are set in motion: The family members and therapist begin to evaluate one another and begin to form a therapeutic alliance, the family is introduced to the therapy process, the family's complaints and patterns are explored, and goals are set for treatment. This section of the chapter also introduces the Martin family, a recently blended family, which will be followed through each phase of the treatment process. By following one case from the first interview through termination, you will be able to gain a coherent picture of family psychotherapy. A blended family was selected because it is estimated that one child in five under the age of 18 is a stepchild and that this type of family will actually outnumber all other kinds by the year 2000 (Glick & Lin, 1986).

Because of the variety of therapeutic agendas to accomplish and in the interest of clarity, the first interview is divided into the following stages, interwoven with the therapist's treatment notes:

1. initial phone call
2. greeting
3. defining the purpose of the meeting
4. defining the problem
5. moving to a systems definition
6. establishing goals and clarifying an intervention plan

## Initial Phone Call

The Martin family was self-referred. Mrs. Martin made the initial phone call concerning her stepdaughter of one year, Cindy. "Cindy," she said, "has caused increasing problems in our home. We're fighting all the time, and my husband and I are at wit's ends. We don't know what to do anymore. We need help!" With this as an introduction, the therapist scheduled an appointment and awaited the first interview.

## *Greeting*

The Martin family (Mr. and Mrs. Martin, who had been married one year; Mrs. Martin's two children from her first marriage, Robert, 17 years of age, and Karen, 11; and 14-year-old Cindy, Mr. Martin's daughter from his first marriage) arrived on time and was sitting quietly in the waiting room. As the therapist introduced himself, Mrs. Martin was the first to rise to shake his hand. She turned and quickly introduced her husband, who extended his hand, and then the children, Robert, Karen, and Cindy, who each nodded to one degree or another. More noticeably, as the children walked past the therapist to his office, Robert looked the therapist in the eye and extended his hand, Karen giggled as she went by, and Cindy followed with stooped shoulders while staring at the floor.

With individual chairs arranged in a circle, the therapist asked the family members to sit wherever they wished. Mrs. Martin pointed to the chairs for Robert and Karen to sit in, while Mr. Martin waited hesitantly for Cindy to choose her seat. Lingering in the doorway, Cindy moved to the chair closest to the door and pushed it farther into the corner. Mr. Martin then took the remaining seat.

After everyone was seated, the therapist began by asking global family questions:

**Therapist:**   Did you have any trouble finding the office? Were my directions clear?

Then he began to contact each of the children individually, going from youngest to oldest:

**Therapist:**   Let me get all the names right. You're Karen, aren't you? How old are you? Where do you go to school?

Completing this process, the therapist next addressed Mrs. Martin and then Mr. Martin.

### *TREATMENT NOTES*

Even during the initial phone call, an observant therapist is already gathering data. Which parent called? Is this the spokesperson for the family? Is this the most motivated parent?

Likewise, in the initial contact in the waiting room, the family members have begun to present themselves to the therapist. Mrs. Martin continues her leadership role in the family. Mr. Martin follows his wife's lead. Robert mirrors his mother's behavior. Karen appropriately reveals her anxiety with her giggle. Cindy's nonverbal behavior clearly pronounces that she does not want to be there and expects the worst in the next hour.

The family members' choice of seating continues their presentation. Mrs. Martin strategically places her children to the left of her. Mr. Martin appears torn between his wife and daughter. Cindy, partly out of protest and partly out of fear, avoids entering the room until the last moment and then proceeds to physically extricate herself from the family circle.

For the therapist's part, he attempts to welcome the family members and allow them to catch their breath by asking global conversational questions. Although the conversation may seem like chit-chat, it serves the valuable function of reducing the family's initial anxiety.

Next, each family member is contacted individually. Notice that the therapist moves from youngest child up to the parents. This serves several purposes. First, individual members are acknowledged. Secondly, the concept of family systems is introduced by avoiding moving directly to Cindy, the identified problem; Cindy is addressed as the second youngest family member and not as the focal point for the meeting. Third, by talking with Karen, the youngest, first, the therapist is giving the older family members the opportunity to observe him: "Does he seem friendly? Will I be comfortable talking to him? Will he ask probing questions? Do I need to be defensive with him?" Finally, Mrs. Martin is the first parent addressed because she originally contacted the therapist: "Mrs. Martin, I guess it's your turn, since we've already talked on the phone."

Overall, the purpose of the greeting stage is to acknowledge the family members and make them somewhat comfortable in the office before moving on to the task at hand. Notwithstanding, one errs by spending too much time in the greeting. The family has come for a purpose and is confused if this is not soon addressed. More specifically, research has shown that a lack of structuring in the early treatment sessions is one factor associated with deterioration in clients' conditions during family therapy (Gurman, Kniskern, & Pinsof, 1986). Thus, a brief greeting stage followed by a structuring of the interview communicates to the family that the therapist is moving purposefully.

## Defining the Interview

As was underlined earlier, the Martin family brought a great deal of anxiety to the first interview. Not only were the family members in pain, but to expose their pain to an outsider in a setting they did not understand was even more unsettling. Consequently, by providing a format, the therapist structured the meeting and reduced to some degree the family's anxiety of the unknown:

**Therapist:**   The chief purpose of this meeting is to give all of you the opportunity to meet me, and vice versa. I understand that a lot has been occurring in your family that has been upsetting for all of you. What I would like to do in this first meeting is to hear everyone's point of view about what's been going on. Finally, at the end of our meeting, I would like to share with you my perceptions, give you my recommendations, and allow time for you to ask me questions.

### TREATMENT NOTES

On a content level, the therapist is laying out the progression of the interview. On a process level, he is again underlining the family theme and a respect for individual perspectives. He is emphasizing that there are many sides to a story (circular causality) and that each member is encouraged to share his or hers. Finally, on the process level, he is trying to form a reciprocal, therapeutic alliance by welcoming the family's questions. In doing so, he is inviting the family members to actively participate in the treatment process and is communicating that therapy is not something that will be done *to* the family; rather, the family members will be contributors in shaping the process.

## Defining the Problem

At this point the therapist directed the meeting to the task at hand. Here he was interested in each family member's perspective on the problem: "Why has each of you come to this meeting?" As well as telling their sides of the story, in this initial step the family members were presenting their viewpoints: Who is to blame? What rules or values has that person violated? How has the family tried to rectify the problem?

**Therapist:** I'd like to find out what you each thought about coming here today and why do you think you're here. Who would like to start?

**Mrs. Martin:** We need to come because we've got to get Cindy straightened out. As I told you on the phone, Cindy has been increasingly angry around the house. We have to ask her twenty times to do something, and even then we end up arguing. On top of that, her school work is the pits.

**Mr. Martin:** Well, I guess coming is a good idea because anything would be an improvement. There's continual fighting around our house. My wife and daughter are always at it.

**Robert:** I came because Mom made the appointment. We're here because of Cindy.

**Karen** [giggling and quickly looking at her mother]: I don't know. I guess because of the fights.

**Cindy** [pointing to her stepmother]: I don't know. Ask her.

After the initial opening by the therapist and the family members' responses, each participant was asked to expand his or her view of the problem. Mrs. Martin began by delineating what she saw as Cindy's disruptive behavior. From her perspective, Mrs. Martin had tried over the previous year to be a combination friend and mother to Cindy. On any number of occasions she had tried to talk with her to find out what was bothering her, but Cindy rebuffed her attempts. Mrs. Martin saw Cindy as having a "bad attitude" at home that was increasingly mirrored in poor school performance. Mrs. Martin, who felt she had tried her level best to help Cindy, wanted Cindy changed.

Mr. Martin explained that Cindy had lived with her mother for several years after the divorce (Cindy's parents were divorced four years before) but that increasing arguments between Cindy and her mother had led to Cindy choosing to live with her father. Mr. Martin had high hopes that he and his new wife could give Cindy the stable home she had lost when the divorce occurred. He could identify the guilt he felt—"Perhaps the divorce is still effecting Cindy"—and his divided loyalties—"I wish my wife and Cindy could get along so that I wouldn't feel so much in the middle." He wanted the fighting to end.

From all accounts, Robert had moved smoothly through adolescence. (His father had died years earlier, but Robert evidenced little signs of unresolved grief.) He was doing well in school, participated in sports, and was active socially. He was a stable support for his mother and was happy she had remarried. Because he was out of the house more than he was in it, he was the most peripheral to the conflicts. He did not feel he had to support or defend his mother in the arguments but wished they were not occurring. Robert wanted to remain on the periphery of the battleground—he had agreed to come to the session only at his mother's insistence—but thought Cindy needed to "get her act together."

Karen also was doing well in school, but Mrs. Martin thought she was beginning to see a change in her attitude. (Her secret fear was that Cindy would influence Karen.) What appeared to the therapist to be predictable preadolescent behavior on Karen's part—for example, beginning to challenge her mother's rules—was interpreted by Mrs. Martin as Cindy's influence. Karen, too, did not want to be brought into the fray but was bothered by her mother's accusation that Cindy was influencing her.

Initially, Cindy sat silently smoldering. When asked her view of the problem, she grudgingly responded, "I don't know." However, as the therapist prodded her to speak, Cindy opened up: "My stepmother is way too strict. She expects people to jump whenever she says so. She's always on my back. She never picks on the other two, only me." Cindy wanted to be left alone.

At this point the therapist opened up the meeting, "Would anyone like to add to or correct what someone else said?" After a brief silence, Mrs. Martin pursued Cindy: "What do you mean I pick on you? You never do anything around the house." With this, the fuse was lit, and the conflict soon erupted in the office. Mrs. Martin and Cindy went head-to-head while each watched Mr. Martin out of the corner of her eye. Robert tightened his jaw, and Karen shifted uneasily in her chair.

## TREATMENT NOTES

Seemingly a straightforward question-and-answer procedure, defining the problem further explores the family's motivation, begins to build a feedback loop between the therapist and family, invites the family to test the therapeutic limits, and may challenge the therapist's capacity to listen and "hear" what is being said.

First, the level of motivation is tested by asking the family members why they came to the meeting. Who wanted the meeting? Who was the driving force to have the session? Who did not want to come? Who couldn't care less one way or another? Who came willingly? Who was pressured into coming? What type of pressure was employed (threat of punishment, guilt, pleading)?

Also, asking all members why they think they are there reveals more of the family's communication style. What was each member told about the purpose of the meeting? Was the communication direct and honest—"We are going because of the problems in this family"—or indirect, confused, or vague—"It doesn't matter why we're going; the man wants us all to be there."

Finally, by throwing the question out to the family as a whole, the therapist is inviting a spokesperson to step forward. This family member is typically the one who possesses the clearest definition of the problem, at least in his or her own mind. Likewise, the spokesperson is probably the one who initiated the contact to begin with and the one most motivated for change. The question, though, is what to change. Rarely does the spokesperson speak of changing the family; rather, someone needs changing, and you can be assured it is not the speaker. Regardless, the spokesperson is the one who brought the family in and, in all probability, will be the one to bring the family back for another session. Consequently, family engagement possibilities increase as the spokesperson becomes engaged with the therapist.

As was mentioned in the first chapter, feedback loops are cycles of communication. Feedback modifies feedback modifies feedback. The family has long-standing and well-established feedback patterns: who talks to whom about what with what effect. In engaging the system, the therapist enters the family's feedback loop and begins to modify it with his own feedback (communication) to the family. As the alliance is coalescing, the therapeutic system (family + therapist) begins to establish its own feedback loops (the collaborative effort).

By asking each member his or her point of view, for example, the therapist is communicating the importance of everyone's experience. Likewise, a communication norm is being established under which everyone's opinion will be heard and valued. This may not be a pattern outside of the therapy setting—and probably is not for many families experiencing difficulties—but at least in the therapist's office this norm will be firmly imposed.

Individually engaging the family members is also an attempt on the therapist's part to develop a basic empathy for the separate perceptions: What is it like in your shoes? Even though the therapist is viewing the family from a systems perspective, the family is still a group of individuals, each of whom will decide: "Can I trust this person [the therapist]? Will he listen to me? Will he try to understand my perspective? Do I want to share anything with him?" Thus, engagement occurs on a person-to-person level first.

A key to establishing person-to-person engagement is to make sure that all words and phrases used by clients are given an explicit meaning. For instance, at one point Mrs. Martin refers to Cindy as having a "bad attitude." If the therapist left the term unchallenged or unclarified, there would be the possibility of six different interpretations. Instead, he asks Mrs. Martin to define the term:

**Therapist:**   I'm not sure what you mean by Cindy's "bad attitude." Would you give me some examples?

**Mrs. Martin:**   Well, she always challenges what I say and never just quietly obeys.

Notice that with this question, the therapist has begun to redefine the problem as existing between people and not within a person. Also, defining the problem becomes an interactive process between the therapist and the family members. And finally, the therapist, in the process of asking clarifying questions, is establishing feedback loops:

**Therapist**   [in response to Mrs. Martin's definition of a bad attitude]: Let me get this straight, and tell me if I'm wrong, but you believe Cindy is being deliberately disrespectful when she questions your decisions?

In phrasing the question in such a manner, the therapist is a win-win position. If he is accurate in his impression, Mrs. Martin agrees and feels understood. If she disagrees, the therapist responds: "I'm sorry. I guess I missed hearing you. Let's try again, because it's important for me to understand your dilemma." Here, the therapist's inaccurate empathy is used to foster further feedback loops with Mrs. Martin and, hopefully, facilitate the engagement process.

## Moving to a Systems Definition

After exploring each family member's definition of the problem, the therapist was in a position to underline the differences and move to a systems definition. Such a definition highlights the interpersonal aspects of the problem and hints at circular causality. To begin to accomplish this, the therapist asked the family members to comment on the *differences* between their perceptions:

**Therapist:** Mr. Martin, your wife says she believes that both of you should hold the line and avoid Cindy's manipulation, but you at times seem to hold a different opinion. I wonder if you could explain this difference of views between the two of you and how both of you deal with it.

With this question, the therapist moved away from the focal conflict to the marital subsystem.

**Therapist:** Mrs. Martin, you and Cindy certainly see things in different ways. Has this always been the case, and if not, when did it begin?

A therapeutic assumption was made that if this conflict had existed from day 1, Mrs. Martin would have been reluctant to remarry. In all probability, the relationship between Cindy and herself was at least cordial in the beginning and only soured at some later point. With the above question, the therapist was seeking out a time when a positive relationship existed between the two and was further seeking to learn whether a specific event or theme led to the disruption.

**Therapist:** Cindy, the differences with your stepmother are clear, but I was wondering if you have differences of opinion with other family members?

Again, rather than rehashing a litany of complaints between Cindy and her stepmother, the therapist redirected Cindy's attention to other family members. First, this was to defuse the focal conflict; second, Cindy's opinions of what others had said were equally important; and finally, she was invited to participate as an equal to other family members and not as the scapegoat.

**Therapist:** Robert, you seem to me to be very observant. It looks as if you pick up a great deal more than you comment on. I wonder if you could tell me what you observed in the last few minutes.

This was a nonthreatening invitation for Robert to participate in therapy.

**Therapist:** Karen, I thought you looked a little worried when your mother and sister were arguing. I wonder if you'd tell me what you were thinking about at that time.

Again, an invitation was extended, but more importantly, the therapist was exploring to what extent Karen would agree or deny that she was worried. If Karen agreed, she would be supplying evidence that the entire family was reacting to the arguments. If she denied being worried and, even more so, denied any feelings concerning the arguments, this would be a strong indication of the family's capacity to deny feelings and would hint at a rigid pattern that would perpetuate a scapegoat.

All of the above questions were analogous to a fishing expedition: You never know when you will get a bite. For instance, some of the questions might result in a blank stare, a shrug of a shoulder, and an "I don't know." You hope that one or two would open the door to exploring the differences among people and their views of one another. Furthermore, by exploring or at least questioning the differences among family members, the therapist shifted the interview from the static blame game to a more fluid focus on interactions: How do you differ? How do you explain the differences? When did the differences appear? How do you manage them? How destructive do they get?

As the interpersonal dynamics became the focus of the interview, it was possible to ascribe a systems definition to the family problems:

**Therapist:**   From what all of you have told me, the fights between Mrs. Martin and Cindy have not always been there. In fact, at one time the two of you got along fine. Something has obviously changed that. I think part of our job is to figure out what happened and how to make it different.

**Therapist:**   From what I have heard, one difficulty that exists is the difference of opinion between the parents over when to pull in the reins and when to trust Cindy's judgment. I believe it must be difficult to draw this line, and sometimes you're bound to disagree. A problem, though, is that Cindy receives mixed messages. Sometimes she gets a green light, and other times it's red. Sometimes her stepmother disagrees with her behavior, while at the same time her father approves of it. It seems to me that it would be helpful if a consistent agreement could be reached, both for the two of your sake and for Cindy's.

**Therapist:**   I'm not sure if all of you have noticed it, and tell me if I'm wrong, but a pattern seems to appear consistently. A disagreement occurs between Cindy and Mrs. Martin; it escalates without resolution; Mr. Martin enters to try to resolve the matter and prevent further arguing, while Robert and Karen are emotionally involved spectators.

**Therapist:**   It's evident that this last year has been a very painful time for all of you, and from what you've told me, it has affected each of you differently. Each of you also seems to have a unique perspective on the problems. Because of this I will need all of your inputs if we are to reduce the tension in the family.

As you can see, underlying all of the above systems definitions was the movement from individual blame to interpersonal dynamics. At this stage of the first interview, what the therapist believed was sometimes irrelevant to what the family believed. It should be remembered that in the engagement process the therapist and family were forming a therapeutic system. Consequently, some type of consensus needed to be reached among all of the participants on the nature of the problem or at least how to approach it. The therapist was only able to "sell" his point of view to the extent that the family was willing to "buy" it. On the other hand, if the therapist has been busy trying to teach the family or fit it into a specific theoretical model—"Your family is poorly differentiated." "Your family possesses poor interpersonal boundaries." "We need to improve the executive subsystem in the family." "You're projecting your family-of-origin issues onto your daughter"—then the family members might feel confused, misunderstood, talked down to, or even irritated, which would lead them to the inevitable question: "What does this have to do with Cindy's bad attitude?"

In moving the Martin family to a systems definition of its problems, the therapist was applying one of the key "arts" of family therapy: the ability to translate his theoretical model into concrete realities that fit the family's world view. For example, one of the first clinical impressions that struck the therapist was the dysfunctional triangle involving the parents and Cindy. Cindy was clearly a focal point of the parents' inability to effectively co-parent, which raised questions of to what extent Mr. and Mrs. Martin had formed a parental unit and hinted at possible marital conflicts. (Mrs. Martin, for instance, might have been furious at the lack of support she was receiving from her husband).

It would have served little purpose, however, for the therapist to expound on his wonderful conceptual understanding of the family's dynamics. Rather, this hypothesis needed to be translated into concrete terms. Of the four examples given above, the second systems definition struck a responsive chord. Mrs. Martin welcomed the opportunity to discuss the co-parenting dynamics in hopes of gaining more support from her husband. By including all the family members in the definition of the problem and potential solution, the therapist was offering hope to the parents that their differences could be resolved and freeing Cindy from a scapegoat position. At this point, with a consensus reached over the definition of the problem, the family was willing to pursue further this "therapy business."

### TREATMENT NOTES

Until this stage of the engagement process, the interview has progressed smoothly. The family members have been happy to tell their sides of the story and have welcomed the therapist's attentive ear. In moving to a systems definition, however, the family's resistance to change is first encountered, with the members attempting to seduce the therapist into playing a supportive role in the drama. Although the concept of resistance will be further elaborated upon in a later chapter, its appearance in the initial phase of treatment highlights several clinical concerns.

Long-standing family patterns are an outgrowth of the Martin family's world view, or paradigm. Even if unsatisfying, they provide the family members with security, predictability, and a sense that they are acting "right" (Anderson & Stewart, 1983). Consequently, the family members enter therapy with their unique views of the problem, and sometimes the members' opinions coalesce around a central theme: Cindy's behavior needs to change.

From a systems perspective, the family's view of the problem becomes more important than the problem itself. For example, as long as Cindy stays within her scapegoat role—a collusion among her and the rest of the family—other aspects of the family's functioning—for example, Mr. and Mrs. Martin's co-parenting capacity—go unnoticed. The more rigidly maintained this view of the problem, the more rigid everyone's roles and the family's patterns become: Cindy feels blamed and victimized and in her anger acts out more; Mrs. Martin is overwhelmed in her efforts to parent Cindy and fears her stepdaughter's influence on her own children; Mr. Martin is torn between his daughter and his new wife; Robert and Karen blame Cindy and just want to be left alone. With these beliefs in place, the Martins continue to ride the merry-go-round.

For the family, the merry-go-round may be an up and down ride going nowhere, but at least it is a known and familiar ride. When the therapist enters the picture, he initially, and briefly, rides the ride until he becomes familiar with its unique rhythms. But then he steps off and attempts to point out other rides the Martins can go on. The Martins, however, have ridden the merry-go-round so long that they do not want to get off, and besides, the therapist appears to be looking at a terrifying, triple-loop roller coaster (potential parenting or marital problems).

Concretely, in the engagement process, a family may resist the therapist's systems definition of the problem: "What do these questions about our parenting and marriage have to do with Cindy's bad attitude?" At this point, the therapist needs to rethink the definition:

- Does the family not understand my definition?
- Have I missed something, and am I therefore off the track?
- Is my definition being resisted because it does not fit the family's experience?
- Is it too threatening a definition for the family to adopt at this time?
- What makes this definition too threatening to the family?
- Is there another way to phrase the definition?

With these questions, the therapist is looking inward—"Have I missed a key experience of the family or poorly phrased my definition?"—and outward—"What is so threatening to the family?"

Because a systems definition is a cooperative effort, a therapist errs by insisting on his or her definition. Therapists who push their viewpoints may believe and take pride in the fact that they are "telling it like it is" but are surprised when families fail to make or cancel follow-up appointments. More to the point, successful engagement is dependent upon the family's willingness to cooperate. The members need to feel listened to and to share in the therapist's definition of the problem. From this solid foundation, the chances of treatment success increase.

## *Establishing Goals and Clarifying an Intervention Plan*

As was mentioned above, minimal structuring of early treatment sessions has been reliably associated with a deterioration in treatment effectiveness (Gurman et al., 1986). Other crucial factors influencing a successful therapeutic outcome are the therapist's encouragement of client initiative and clients' assumption of an active role in resolving their problems (Orlinsky & Howard, 1986). With this in mind, the systems definition constructed between the therapist and the family lays the foundation for establishing the goals of therapy.

Goals for therapy for the Martin family might range from straightforward symptom relief (less fighting in the home) to more global objectives (improved communication, improved self-esteem, a better attitude) and should be established in a collaborative manner. Still, the broader the goals the therapist and family set, the easier it will be to lose sight of them in the give and take of therapy sessions. Without a clear focus, frustration may develop, and family members may legitimately ask: "Where are we going? Are we getting anywhere?" The therapist proceeded this way:

**Therapist:** If our sessions are going to be worthwhile, it's important for us to reach an agreed-upon goal. Would you each tell me what you'd like to get out of our meetings, and I'll also tell you my opinions.

The therapist thus began collaborative effort of reaching consensus on therapeutic goals.

Each family member expressed in one form or another his or her own personal goals. Mr. Martin wanted a decrease in the arguments. Mrs. Martin also wanted fewer arguments and felt that Cindy's "bad attitude" needed to change for that to happen. Cindy wanted her parents to quit picking on her and leave her alone. Robert wanted the fights to end. Karen said she did not know!

**Therapist:** Well, there is clearly a variety of goals. But despite these differences a common theme appears to be a desire to decrease the tension in the home by reducing the arguments. I think this is a workable goal. But I think it would be helpful to know when we have achieved this goal. How would we know that we have reached our goal?

Rather than leaving the goals as abstractions, the therapist tried to define them in more specific and concrete terms.

**Therapist:** While we're discussing goals, I'd also like to hear what positive things are going on in the family and your ideas on increasing them.

More often than not, goals are stated in terms of reducing negatives. The opposite side of the same coin, however, is an identification of what is positive in the family and how to increase those behaviors.

From a systems perspective, the goals are interpersonal in nature. Nevertheless, a family member may state an intrapersonal goal:

**Mr. Martin:** I want to feel at peace in my own home.

While certainly legitimate, intrapersonal goals are easily translated into systems goals:

**Therapist:** Mr. Martin, I can understand your desire for peace in your home. What do you believe you need to do to make this happen?

Again the therapist refocused on the family and the responsibility of each family member to change it.

Ideally, therapeutic goals flow directly from the systems definition of the problem. It is important to define these goals in soluble terms that involve the family members. A key to doing this is to change nouns into verbs. For example, Cindy's "bad attitude" (a static, intrapersonal term) was translated into improving the relationship between Cindy and her parents (a fluid, interpersonal goal) on which all the family members could agree.

Accepting "changing Cindy's attitude" as the goal would probably have doomed therapy from the start. A person either has or does not have a bad attitude. Consequently, therapy would have been attempts to discern Cindy's attitude: Is it bad or not? Has it changed or not? Obviously this effort would only have further maintained the family's basic scapegoating patterns.

By instead defining a goal as improving relationships, the therapist and family members involved everyone in the solution. Cindy alone did not have to change—an idea she found revolting and would have fought against with all her might—but instead the family relationships became the focus of treatment. As a family, the Martins agreed to begin family therapy with the stated goal of decreasing the tension in their home by reducing the number of arguments.

## TREATMENT NOTES

Clarifying the intervention plan is the final issue addressed in the first interview. Specifically, the intervention plan is the rough skeleton of the treatment process: how long do the sessions last? How frequently will we meet? How many sessions will we have?

Because of the legacy of individual psychotherapy's "50-minute hour," weekly, one-hour sessions have evolved as an acceptable pattern for family therapy. Nevertheless, no set standard exists. Rather, intervention plans are the result of many factors: time and financial limitations of both the therapist and family, the goals of therapy, and the therapist's theoretical position.

For example, some therapists may operate within settings, that is, clinics, HMO's, that emphasize short-term, brief treatment. Five to ten sessions may be the acceptable standard. In other situations the family's financial and insurance coverage may limit the number or frequency of the sessions. The goals of therapy may be short- or long-term and may reflect the therapist's theoretical position or family's needs. Thus, the exact nature of the intervention plan is unique for each case. With some families, the therapist may meet weekly or bi-weekly for an hour, while with others the intervention plan involves monthly two-hour sessions.

The luxury of experimenting with time and frequency enhances one's therapeutic options. You may find that the first interview consistently takes one-and-a-half hours or that longer family sessions spaced further apart make more sense. Experimentation teaches what works best. As a beginning family therapist you may want to experiment with different time schedules. Some therapists find an hour too short a time period for a family session. Others find that working with families intensely for two or three hours spaced over longer periods of time suits them better.

In keeping with the tone of the book, the design of the treatment plan is a conjoint effort between the therapist and the family members. With the Martin family, weekly, hour-long sessions were agreed to for several reasons. First, the family was in a moderate crisis state. The arguments were becoming more frequent and intense and relief was needed. Second, weekly sessions would allow for a continuity of treatment to develop. The arguments were based in the struggle to form a new stepfamily, and building a solid foundation for a stepfamily would take time and consistency. Third, the family's work and financial restraints would only allow for weekly sessions. Finally, because the goal of reducing the arguments was clearly stated and thus serve as an end-point, the number of sessions was left open-ended.

## Summary

If it was managed well, the first interview has resulted in a tentative therapeutic alliance between the therapist and family, and the family patterns have begun to be discerned. From the therapist's perspective, he or she gains an appreciation of each of the family members, forms early working hypotheses concerning the system's dynamics, reaches consensus with the family on a definition of the problem, and proposes an intervention plan. The family members, ideally, feel that they have been listened to and understood, have an initial sense of trust in the therapist, and view the intervention plan as a reasonable one.

In order to facilitate the engagement process, Table 2.1 presents a series of questions as guidelines.

## Table 2.1    *Questions Guiding the First Interview*

### Reasons for Referral

1. Why is the family seeking treatment at this time?
2. Are the family members in agreement on their problems?
3. What is the level of motivation in the family to pursue therapy?
4. Are outside referral sources involved? What is the relationship between the family and the referral source?

### Family's Agenda for the Therapist

1. What role or roles do family members expect the therapist to play? Judge? Referee? Ally? Savior?
2. Are alliances sought by individual family members? What are those agendas?

### Greeting Process

1. Who is the spokesperson for the family?
2. Who appears to have the power in the family? To whom do family members look when they are speaking?
3. Who brought the family into therapy? What is that person's agenda? Will this person decide if the family will continue in treatment?
4. Who are the motivated family members? Are they seeking help for themselves or to change another family member?

### Defining the Problem

1. How does the family define its problem?
2. Is one person blamed for the family's difficulties? How long has the blaming been going on? How rigid is this paradigm? Is there family consensus on this point?
3. How willing are the family members to examine other possible explanations?
4. Does the family's definition of the problem suppress potential, threatening anxiety?

### Developing a Systems Definition

1. What differences are identifiable in the family members' presentations?
2. What differences do the family members recognize? How are these differences managed?
3. What differences and potential conflicts are denied or rejected?
4. What resistance is evoked with the attempted shift to a system's definition? What is the basis of the resistance? What fears are being provoked?

### *Table 2.1*   *Questions Guiding the First Interview*

5. What systems definition will be acceptable to both the therapist and family members and will permit the establishment of feasible goals?

**Planning Interventions**

1. What interventions will the family accept?
2. What interventions will push the family's anxiety past manageable limits?
3. On what family strengths can the intervention plan be built?

### Treatment Notes

**Triangles and Scapegoating**
1. What triangles are central to the family's problems?
2. In what ways are the triangles created?
3. Does scapegoating exist in the family?
4. What purpose does the scapegoat serve?

**Boundaries and Coalitions**
1. How clearly defined and maintained are the family's boundaries?
2. What boundaries are enmeshed and/or disengaged?
3. Do cross-generational coalitions exist in the family?

**Power and Control**
1. Who controls the family? How do they control the family? Guilt? Forcefulness? Coercion? Threats?
2. Are alliances with the therapist sought opposing other family members?
3. Who will challenge the therapist's control of the sessions? How will this person do so?

**Intimacy**
1. How is intimacy expressed in the family?
2. What interpersonal distance exists between family members?
3. Are certain family members expressing a greater desire for intimacy than others?
4. How are requests for intimacy managed?

**Communication**
1. Do family members speak to one another directly? Who speaks to whom? Are the messages clearly sent?
2. Do family members interrupt one another? Who interrupts whom?
3. Do family members listen when someone else is talking? Who is listened to and who is not?

# *Glossary*

**Inappropriate coalitions**   Alliances formed across subsystem boundaries, resulting in an imbalance of power.

**Intimacy**   The capacity to form caring, expressive, affective bonds while respecting individual boundaries.

**Power**   The ability to influence others.

**Triangulation**   Diffusion of dyadic conflict by expanding the relationship to include a third person (child, therapist, and so on).

# Engagement Phase I: Establishing Therapeutic Boundaries

**The Therapeutic alliance: Conceptual notes**
**Case presentation**
**Treatment notes**
**Summary**

Although initiated in the first interview, the **therapeutic alliance** between the therapist and family is more firmly established in the first several sessions. In this alliance, the family and therapist evolve a basic level of trust, a working relationship, and a shared agenda—that is, an agreed-upon definition of the problem and treatment plan. Bordin (1982) refers to the relationship between the therapist and client(s) as a "working alliance" made up of three parts: (1) a consensus between therapist and client on the goals of therapy, (2) an agreement and collaboration on the relevance and implementation of various therapeutic tasks, and (3) a strong, positive affective bond between therapist and client.

In the family therapy literature, the process of forming a therapeutic alliance has been referred to by any number of terms—for example, *establishing rapport* and *joining*—but a description of the "how-to" of this process varies depending upon one's theoretical model.

For example, Minuchin (1974) describes it in terms of a joining and accommodating process. Joining emphasizes the therapist's actions in response to the family system and requires that the therapist accommodate (flexibly adapt) to the family's patterns and styles of relating. Thus, from Minuchin's model, a successful engagement process is heavily dependent upon the therapist's capacity to respond and adapt to the family.

At the other end of the spectrum, Whitaker and Keith (1981) argue that the therapist does not have a choice in joining the family. Rather, the family's willingness to continue the treatment sessions indicates that the therapist has already been assigned a role in the family drama (for example, judge, savior, ally). Nevertheless, they do add that to complete the joining process, the therapist must develop a basic empathy with the family.

The first section of this chapter discusses the engagement process from a conceptual point of view and is divided into three interrelated parts: (1) family inputs, including background and values; (2) the therapist's inputs, including life patterns and training; and (3) the role of the therapist. In the following section, case material is presented, and then the pragmatic issues of establishing therapeutic boundaries are addressed.

# The Therapeutic Alliance: Conceptual Notes

## Family Inputs

As a social group, a family brings to therapy a host of factors: generational ties from two extended families, historical references—a sense of past, present, and future—and an established repertoire of values, norms, roles, and interactive patterns. Two primary issues in the family therapy literature are the influence of ethnicity and the family's stage in the life cycle.

### Ethnicity

Viewed from a systems perspective, a family is not a self-contained unit operating autonomously but a subsystem of broader community and cultural systems. Just as the strength of family therapy is the ability to place an individual's symptoms within a family context, family patterns can also be placed within a broader cultural context. This broader cultural context is the family's ethnic heritage, a heritage steeped in norms and values transmitted over generations, norms and values that provide an identity for the family members and also guidelines for behavior.

Because ethnicity provides a sense of belonging and historical continuity, McGoldrick, Pearce, and Giordano (1982) argue that it is a powerful influence on the individuals in a family. Specifically related to treatment, they point out that family stresses are compounded when ethnic stresses or transitions interact with life cycle transitions. For example, parents with strong ethnic values that foster mutual dependency among family members may clash strongly with an emerging adolescent who adopts peer-related values of autonomy. Likewise, for some people the influence of members of an extended ethnic family is a powerful force in the nuclear family's life. What extended family members will think and how they will react are frequently important factors in a nuclear family's problem-solving ability.

To use a more concrete example, Nancy Boyd-Franklin (1987, 1989) has written extensively on black families in therapy. She observes that because the traditional sources of help have been extended family members, very close friends, and church leaders and because of the legacy of racism, black families may be extremely reluctant to enter treatment. Therapy may be seen as intrusive and as another labeling process of the establishment: "We will be told we are crazy." Consequently, empowering the black family and mobilizing the family's ability to successfully interact with external systems are key therapeutic goals.

Regardless of the specifics, ethnicity may powerfully shape and control family members' behavior. Reiss (1981), for instance, speaks of the family's capacity to construct its own view of reality: a **family paradigm** that guides the behavior of the family members and serves as a guideline for making sense of the world. Certainly, the threads of ethnicity reinforce the paradigm.

For example, the simple statement "We are a *close* family" may have extremely divergent meanings when the word *close* is further defined. For a strong ethnic family, closeness may be a primary motivational force. Extended family members live in close proximity; Sunday dinner at the grandmother's house is mandatory; and in-laws may consistently feel outside of the large, blood-related extended family. Still, for another family, the definition of closeness is "Well, we see them about three times a year and call about once a month, but you always know they're there for you."

With the possibility of such diverse definitions, a clinician errs in ascribing any meanings without first understanding the family's ethnic paradigm. Words such as *love, close, distant, hurt,* and *anger* have specific meanings for each family. Consequently, it behooves the therapist to discover what these words mean for a particular family. Not only is the therapist gaining valuable knowledge of the family's functioning, but also the process of engagement is enhanced because the family members sense that the therapist is attempting to understand them.

In the Martin family, Mrs. Martin grew up in a traditional Italian family. Being from the second generation of the family in the United States (both her parents immigrated from Italy), she combined traditional Italian values with middle-class American ones. From her framework, children were closely guided and protected, and above all else, they *respected their parents.* Cindy's behavior was a clear affront to her stepmother's values. To compound the matter, Mr. Martin was third-generation Irish and had allowed his daughter much more freedom than would ever be allowed in an Italian family. Thus, a clash in values was one of the cracks in the stepfamily's foundation.

Besides clashes within the family, potential differences exist between the therapist's and family's ethnic paradigms. Spiegel (1982) points out that no matter what their ethnic origins, middle-class therapists have been socialized in terms of mainstream values: The therapist expects clients to keep appointments, be motivated to change, and work at therapeutic tasks. More specifically, personal autonomy is emphasized over emotional dependency. These values may be at odds with the family's values. And in this clash, the therapy often suffers. For example, members of a strong, traditional ethnic family who value emotional dependency on one another will quickly and unilaterally terminate treatment with a therapist who is pushing autonomy.

### Family Life Cycle

As mentioned above, family stresses may also be compounded by life cycle transitions (McGoldrick et al., 1982). If we view the family as a system moving through time, transition and change are inevitable. This developmental perspective assumes that there are tasks at each stage that need to be accomplished and that the transition from one stage to another is always accompanied by a normal degree of crisis (Preto & Travis, 1985). Furthermore, symptoms may appear in any stage of development and may signal a difficulty that a family is experiencing in negotiating that particular stage.

For example, Carter and McGoldrick (1988) outline six stages of the **family life cycle:**

1. leaving home: single young adults
2. the joining of families through marriage: the new couple
3. families with young children
4. families with adolescents
5. launching children and moving on
6. families in later life

Carter and McGoldrick also identify accompanying emotional processes at each transition and the changes in the family functioning required to proceed developmentally. For instance, the emergence of adolescence in one or more children (as in the Martin family) requires more flexibility in the family's boundaries to include the adolescents' quest for autonomy and a shift in parent-child relationships to permit the adolescents to move in and out of the system.

Through the process of adolescence, the relationship is transformed from parent-child through parent-adolescent to parent–young adult. This developmental change reflects a new balance between individuality and connectedness within the family (Worden, 1991). The adolescent developmentally seeks autonomy and a sense of identity separate from the family but at the same time does not wish a complete cutoff. Employing the family as a home base (stability), the adolescent is then free to explore the world but also return as needed. Combrinck-Graham (1985) captures this fluidity by describing family development as a process of oscillations between centripetal (turning inward) and centrifugal (turning outward) movements. At times family members pull together—for example, at childbirth or illness—whereas at other times individuality and separateness are emphasized—for example, when starting a new job or heading off to college.

Family stress is often greatest at transition points from one stage to another, and symptoms are most likely to appear when there is an interruption of the unfolding life cycle (Carter & McGoldrick, 1988). In particular, divorce and remarriage are two major disruptions of the life cycle and place tremendous strains on the family. In the case of the Martin family, a death of a spouse (Mrs. Martin's first husband), a divorce (Mr. Martin's), and a remarriage laid the groundwork for many of the family's problems.

As a final note, Simon (1988) argues that the therapist's own stage in the life cycle has an impact on the therapy. How the two life cycles combine is an important part of the fit between therapist and family. For example, a therapist who has already moved through the family's current stage of development and its accompanying dilemmas may have personal knowledge of what the family is going through and easily empathize with them. However, the reverse may also be true. Because the therapist moved easily through the stage, he or she may minimize the family's problems. Or worse yet, a therapist in the same stage as the family may be just as stuck there.

In conclusion, a basic understanding and appreciation of the family life cycle greatly enhances the building of the therapeutic alliance. A life cycle approach sensitizes the therapist to developmental issues with which the family may be struggling and suggests initial hypotheses to guide assessment and intervention.

## Therapist's Inputs

Just as the family operates from its own paradigm, the therapist's paradigm is equally strong. Therapists bring to therapy their academic and training experiences, the cultural impact of their gender on their theories and personal experiences, and their own issues involving their family of origin and life cycle. All of these factors shape their own world views and their capacity to form therapeutic alliances with families.

### Theory and Training

Each model of family therapy addresses, to one degree or another, functional and dysfunctional patterns in families, important assessment issues, goal setting and the structure of the therapeutic process, the role of the therapist, techniques unique to the model, and the curative factors in the change process. Nichols and Schwartz (1991) point out that many of the concepts and methods of a family model will be determined by the model's assumptions about people. For example, if power is seen as a key dimension in family life, ways to diffuse and redirect power in the family become paramount. Or if love and intimacy are seen as most strongly influencing family relationships, therapy will focus on the sharing of the members' feelings.

Simply put, each model presents its own world view (paradigm) of family life. Thus, the adoption of any theoretical position reflects a "tightness-of-fit" between the model, the therapist, and the family, particularly in terms of utilitarian value: Do the family data fit the theory? Does the model facilitate the therapist's understanding of the family and guide his or her interventions?

By this stage of your training you have probably been exposed to several of the family therapy models. Some have been exciting and stimulating, and others have appeared vague and confusing. Some have made intuitive sense, whereas others have not matched your experience or personal style.

Despite the potential or probable confusion and uncertainty, the best advice, particular for the beginning family therapist, is to learn one model well. First, knowing one model well provides a reference point with which to compare other models: What are the differences in the models' description of functional and dysfunctional family patterns? What are the differences in the therapist's role in the change process? And so forth.

Secondly, by learning one model well, therapists become consistent when working with families. Each model possesses an internal logic to guide the therapist's actions. This logic serves as a beacon through the strong winds and seas of therapy sessions. Along the same line, consistency on the therapist's part projects to the family a confidence of belief, of "knowing what I am doing." The therapist acts with confidence, which is crucial to engaging the family.

Still, a note of caution needs to be added because as Papp (1983) points out, no one approach is right for all families and situations. This point is further underlined by a review of the research, which found no support for the universal applicability and efficacy of any one family therapy approach (Gurman et al., 1986). Thus, for a beginning family therapist, the best path is to learn a model well while staying open to other viewpoints.

### The Effects of Gender

Directly related to the influence of theory on the therapist's behavior are cultural **gender biases.** Recent critiques argue persuasively that current models of family therapy have been blind to the impact of gender on family functioning as well as on the models themselves (Luepnitz, 1988; Walsh & Scheinkman, 1989). The models have not taken into account the differential in power and status between men and women in the larger social systems in which families are embedded. Thus, all interventions need to allow for the different socialization processes of women and men (Walters, Carter, Papp, & Silverstein, 1988).

Hare-Mustin (1989), for example, has found that many family therapists value differentiation—separating emotions from feelings and clearly establishing interpersonal boundaries—and the negotiation of differences (male-oriented behaviors) as treatment goals while playing down such goals as an increase in caretaking and nurturing (female-oriented behaviors). Systems models that the therapists endorsed frequently reduce the family to an abstract and mechanistic structure while minimizing the value of intuition and feelings. Therapy, consequently, focuses on changing family structure and minimizes feelings.

Newberry, Alexander, and Turner (1991) believe, however, that the family therapist's role requires both instrumental behaviors (goal-directed, assertive, and structuring) and expressive ones (which emphasize creating interpersonal closeness and warmth). In an empirical study they found that male and female family therapy trainees did not differ significantly on the rates of these kinds of behaviors. Interestingly, however, fathers responded more positively to therapy than did mothers when therapists used instrumental behavior—active, goal-directed behavior appealed to the men—and all family members expected gender-stereotypic behavior of male and female therapists. (If the therapist does not carry the gender bias into the session, the family will!)

Further support for the therapist combining instrumental and expressive behaviors is provided by Green and Herget (1991). In their empirical study, families improved more when their therapists were warmer and more actively structuring. It would appear, therefore, that the therapeutic alliance is enhanced when the therapist combines interpersonal warmth and assertive, directive behavior.

To return to the Martin family, gender issues played a large role in the treatment process. For example, the family's chief complaint was the conflict between the stepmother and stepdaughter. From one perspective, Mrs. Martin could be seen as intrusive and controlling, and Cindy could be seen as vying for her father's attention in competition with her stepmother. With this hypothesis the therapist would focus on disengaging Mrs. Martin and allowing Cindy more time with her father—changing the family's structural patterns.

Walters and her colleagues (1988) offer another perspective. They argue that because women are acculturated to move toward emotional issues and not away from them, stepmothers and daughters are drawn together as the family undergoes this transition and new beginning. Moreover, women are socialized to assume responsibility for the family's emotional life. Thus, if the transitions are not going smoothly, women blame themselves and are blamed by others for their supposed failures.

Within this context, Mrs. Martin's behavior is readily understandable. She bore the responsibility to make this new stepfamily work and moved to make it happen. And at the time of the first interview, she bore the shame and guilt for the family conflicts. Clearly, in this situation, the therapist would only compound the family's problems by focusing on her "over-involved and controlling" behavior. She would feel increasing blame and frustration, which would not bode well for change.

### The Therapist's Family of Origin and Life Cycle

Moving away from the development of one's conceptual model and the problems of gender bias, the therapist's own **family of origin** strongly influences the engagement process. Therapists, for better or worse, carry with them the paradigm of their family of origin. This is neither bad nor good but rather a simple fact: They are not immune to the very thing they treat, family systems.

With some families, engagement is relatively easy, with commonalities permitting an immediate rapport. These shared elements may be quite diverse—similar ethnic or religious upbringing, value systems, interests, and life cycle stage—but they are quickly recognized, overtly or covertly, by both the therapist and the family. Subsequently, the therapist "knows" the family, and the family members feel comfortable with someone who they believe will understand them and with a style that reflects their own.

As in most areas, however, there can be too much of a good thing. Although commonalities between the therapist and family increase the probability of engagement, if the family's dynamics mirror the therapist's issues concerning family of origin or life cycle, therapeutic change may be difficult to achieve. For instance, a therapist with an alcoholic father may experience difficulty working with a family which has as a chief issue the effect of the father's alcoholism on the mother and children. Although readily understanding what it is like in the children's shoes, the therapist may have difficulty empathizing with the father. Consequently, lineal causality may enter the picture: "Everything would be better in this family if the father quit drinking." Unfortunately, in this scenario, the father believes that he is being blamed for the family problems and unilaterally terminates therapy.

A similar example is when a young therapist is working with a family with an acting-out adolescent who feels overcontrolled. In these situations, the therapist, recently out of a similar developmental period, may readily appreciate the adolescent's request and work toward changing the parents. With this agenda in the room, the parents sense the blame being sent their way, do not feel understood, and cancel the next appointment with the message "We will call back."

Family therapy theories differ in their emphasis on the need of therapists to explore their own family-of-origin issues. Proponents of Bowen's family systems theory strongly believe that the therapist's own extended family work is a key to developing the therapeutic neutrality to conduct family therapy, whereas structural and strategic models do not believe that it is relevant to becoming a successful family therapist (Titleman, 1987).

Despite these differences, some knowledge and understanding of one's own family paradigm may facilitate the engagement process and save one from falling into the trap of lineal causality. Likewise, it is often grandiose to believe that one can engage any and all families. For instance, although one may easily engage a teenage victim of incest, it may be much more difficult to work with the abusing father. In these situations, where the therapist finds it difficult to engage a family member because of a conflict in value systems, therapy will quickly bog down as the therapist fails to engage the entire family. Hence, a referral elsewhere is needed.

## The Therapist's Role

In forming a therapeutic alliance, is the therapist an outside expert who diagnoses the family and directs it into new behavior? Does the therapist need to merge with the family to fully appreciate its dilemmas? Are family therapists guilty of fitting families into defined theoretical models? And overall, what precisely should the therapist's role be?

Overall, the therapist's model strongly influences the therapeutic process. Moreover, each model's assumptions, at the very least, broadly define the therapist's role. For example, a behavioral family therapist is an objective observer outside of the family system who serves as a "consultant" to parents, who in turn serve as the primary change agents (Falloon, 1986). On the other hand, experiential family therapists use all of their personal reactions to both nurture and confront families (Whitaker & Bumberry, 1988). A consistent theme in the field is to view family therapists as experts who "see" the "real" family dynamics and who "do" things to families. Recently, however, this theme has been challenged.

In a review, Nichols and Schwartz (1991) point out that in the past family therapists too often made the mistake of believing that their models (theories) were describing and identifying "real" family interactions—for instance, that families were highly undifferentiated, that a child's symptoms implied marital conflict, and the like. Instead, family therapy theories have begun to be seen as just that, theories (a coherent group of propositions used as explanations). To this end, a significant contribution has been the constructivist perspective.

Simply put, **constructivist** family therapists argue that what therapists "see" is a product of their particular assumptions about families and their interactions with families (Efran, Lukens, & Lukens, 1990; Keeney & Ross, 1985). Consequently, therapeutic reality is co-constructed by the family and therapist through mutual participation and sharing (Goolishian & Anderson, 1987, 1990). The meaning of the problem, its meaning to the family, and potential solutions are all a product of the interaction between the therapist and the family. Consequently, the therapist is not standing outside the family, an expert ascribing theoretical concepts to the family's functioning or "doing" something to the family. Instead the therapist is involved in a thoroughly collaborative enterprise: a search to discover meaning to the family's problem.

Constructivism represents a radical shift in the assumptions underlying family therapy. (To further understand the philosophical underpinnings of constructivism, see Watzlawick's (1984) book, *The Invented Reality: How Do We Know What We Believe We Know? Contributions to Constructionism.*) The family therapist is not the all-knowing expert assessing and telling the family members what to do. Instead, the process of therapy involves the therapist moving within the family's reality and language toward understanding and changing the assumptions that the members have about their problem (Goolishian & Anderson, 1987, 1990).

The purpose of introducing the constructivist perspective is to alert you to the field's ongoing discussion of this issue and to point out that there is no universally accepted role for the therapist. Role prescriptions vary as theories vary, with a range from viewing the therapist as an outside expert who does things to families to viewing the therapist as co-investigator with the family into the meaning of the family's "reality."

Beginning family therapists, more often than not, start their careers as relative purists—following the model to which they were exposed in graduate school and training—but with increasing experience most gradually become more eclectic (Nichols & Schwartz, 1991). Consequently, the roles that therapists' evolve are frequently an amalgamation of theory, experience, their personality, and personal preference.

With this in mind and keeping with the tone of the book, the rest of the chapter addresses the role of the therapist in building a therapeutic alliance in pragmatic terms: "What do I do in the therapy sessions?" To further this discussion, the role of the therapist is viewed from the perspective of establishing and maintaining therapeutic boundaries and the therapist's use of self in the treatment process.

Before discussing these issues, however, my personal, therapeutic role (or biases?) should be defined (Worden, 1991):

1. The therapist is responsible for promoting an atmosphere conducive to change.
2. In so doing, the therapist actively forms a therapeutic alliance *in collaboration with the family.* Therapy is a conjoint effort between the therapist and family with the therapist as a participant, observer, and facilitator.
3. The therapist may lead or show the way to change through supporting, questioning, challenging, or provoking the family, but he or she gives utmost respect to the family's capacity or willingness to change.
4. Consequently, change is ultimately the responsibility and *choice* of the family.

# Case Presentation

Having agreed to begin family therapy, the Martin family tentatively stuck a toe in the water. Mr. Martin (Peter) worried that the sessions would be too hot to handle. He had actively sought to avoid confrontations at home and was fearful that therapy would bring more of the same. Mrs. Martin (Donna) covertly believed that she was to blame for the family's unhappiness but projected the blame onto Cindy. Cindy assumed that the therapist was going to be just one more adult trying to control her. Robert said clearly that he did not want to be there and sought to be excused from future meetings. And Karen's behavior regressed as the tension in the room built.

One of the most difficult things for anyone to do is to go to a therapist for the first time. Expectations are colored by cultural stereotypes: "Will she be able to read my mind? I will be so vulnerable. Will I be blamed for the problem? Will I discover something I'm afraid of?" But to go with your family is even more unpredictable: "Why are we all going? I wonder what will be said? Will they blame me? Will I say more than I should? Will I say something I'll pay for later." This unpredictability alone raises anxiety and leads to a reluctance in all of the family members.

Frequently underlying these fears is a nagging sense of shame, failure, and blame. This is particularly true for parents with a "troubled" child: "Where have we gone wrong? Why can't we handle this ourselves? Why do we have to go to a shrink? They always blame things on parents. I don't buy any of this psychology stuff."

For these families, therapy is a double-bind encounter: "We [the parents] want help for our son or daughter, but we fear we'll be blamed. Moreover, if the therapist succeeds, that means we're failures as parents. But if the therapy doesn't work, then even an expert was unable to change our child, and we truly have done the best we could given how difficult our child is." This ambivalence, colored by both hopes and fears, may make the engagement process particularly difficult with some families.

As for the Martins, Cindy's and Donna's arguments threatened the very existence of the family. Mr. and Mrs. Martin did not know how much more stress they could take. The stepfamily as a unit was still in its infancy and needed nurturing to grow, not strife.

As a means of summarizing, the following points highlight many of the Martin family's characteristics that are common to stepfamilies with adolescents:

**1.** At the time of divorce, the authority structure of the family is disrupted at the very time the emerging teenager needs clear and firm limits (Keshet & Mirkin, 1985). Cindy entered early adolescence at the height of her parents' conflict that led to their divorce. During this time her parents were absorbed in the dissolution of their marriage, and Cindy lacked consistent limits. To compound the matter, she learned to exploit the differences between her parents to her advantage. She became increasingly manipulative to hide the fear of a scared little girl watching her parents' marriage end.

**2.** In the postdivorce living arrangement, the adolescent has a more intense involvement with the parent he or she lives with, and a typical way of increasing the intensity is through angry exchanges (Keshet & Mirkin, 1985). Cindy originally lived with her mother following her parents' divorce. But their arguments frequently escalated to the point at which Mr. Martin was called by his ex-wife and told: "You have got to do something with your daughter. She's out of control." For Cindy's part, during her visits with her father she complained of her mother's "screaming and yelling." Finally, after a particularly heated exchange, Cindy's mother blurted out, "If you don't like it here, then go live with your father." To which Cindy counterpunched, "I will; anyplace is better than this!" Angry words and stubborn pride are a lethal combination in families. Cindy left the next day for her father's home.

**3.** Girls have a greater difficulty than do boys after a remarriage (Clingempeel, Grand, & Ievoli, 1984; Wallerstein & Kelly, 1980). Cindy liked Donna when Donna and her father were only dating. She felt that her father was lonely much of the time and was glad there was someone with whom he was comfortable. The direct time that Cindy spent with the future Mrs. Martin was minimal because her father usually took Donna out alone. When her father brought up the idea of marriage, Cindy experienced a sick feeling in her stomach. Dating was one thing; marriage was something else. Cindy would now have a stepmother! Boszormenyi-Nagy and Spark (1973) identify loyalty issues as a key ingredient in family life. In their framework, a family member is viewed as embedded in a multiperson loyalty network that demands compliance with the expectations and obligations of the group. There is a responsibility, in other words, to act in prescribed ways toward others. Despite their differences, Cindy felt a loyalty to her mother. She was her mother, and no one would take her place! Cindy could barely tolerate the idea of a stepmother, and when Donna attempted to parent Cindy (that is, discipline and instruct her), it was akin to throwing down the gauntlet. Cindy would have none of it.

**4.** Adolescents have a particularly difficult time with the stepfamily's new discipline structure (Lutz, 1983). In the process of individuation, the movement from a childlike dependency state to increased autonomy and a sense of self, the adolescent's chief tool is to test the family's limits. Any parent of an adolescent or a professional who works with adolescents will tell you that testing limits is the teenager's breakfast of champions. To emerge into adolescence in an intact family is difficult enough—"They still treat me like a child; I want some freedom"—but to have to adapt to a whole new set of rules in a new stepfamily is intolerable.

**5.** Of all the possible relationships, the stepmother-stepdaughter relationship is the most difficult to develop in a stepfamily (Clingempeel et al.,

1984). Moreover, traditional gender roles requiring women to take responsibility for the emotional well-being of the family pit stepmother and stepdaughter against each other (Carter, 1988). As discussed above, Cindy was bound by loyalty to her mother. But equally significantly, she felt a rivalry with Donna, a competition for Peter's attention but also a struggle for control. Cindy would not allow Donna to control or influence her. She was more than happy at any opportunity to ignore or respond passively-aggressively to Donna's requests.

**6.** The adolescent and stepfamily exemplify conflicting periods in the life cycle. The adolescent is seeking to break from dependent parental bonds, whereas the stepfamily is seeking to create bonds and establish new parent-child relationships (Visher & Visher, 1988). Mr. Martin hoped that Cindy would join his new family and that they would all become close. Still guilty over his divorce, he hoped to make amends to Cindy with the new family. Moreover, he saw the opportunity to make a successful second family. Cindy, on the other hand, wanted to be out with friends.

## Treatment Notes

### The Therapeutic Alliance

In forming a therapeutic alliance, the therapist accommodates to the family norms while also drawing the therapeutic boundaries needed for treatment to progress. For example, while engaging the Martin family, the therapist found three issues to be paramount: the fragile nature of newly formed stepfamilies, the need to avoid gender bias in focusing on Mrs. Martin, and the need to understand the family's life cycle.

#### The Fragility of Newly Formed Stepfamilies

The shared history is between the parents and their children and not between the spouses or steprelationships. The newest and weakest bond in the family is between the spouses, and consequently, it is important for the therapist to give a great deal of attention and support to the couple bond (Carter, 1988).

The triangle involving Mr. and Mrs. Martin and Cindy threatens the stepfamily. Mrs. Martin wants to be close to her stepdaughter, but Cindy's behavior is a direct affront to her. Mr. Martin loves his new wife but also loves his daughter. Their conflicts hurt him greatly, and he hopes to avoid having to choose one or the other. In this mismatch, both Mr. and Mrs. Martin are wondering secretly and silently whether getting married was such a good idea.

Thus, in the engagement phase of treatment, the marital dyad is supported and not challenged:

**Therapist:**   It's never easy trying to blend two families together, particularly with teenagers. During these difficult times, how do the two of you [Mr. and Mrs. Martin] support each other?

Here the therapist is emphasizing the ways in which the parents interact positively and not what is driving them apart.

### Avoiding Gender Bias

From a lineal perspective, Mrs. Martin's actions toward Cindy could be labeled intrusive and controlling, making her a "wicked stepmother." But Mrs. Martin is being true to her ethnic tradition and can proudly point to her two children as examples of the correctness of her approach.

Furthermore, she is assuming a great deal of the emotional responsibility in making the stepfamily work. Mr. Martin is colluding with her by encouraging her to make many of the decisions concerning the children while he avoids taking a clear stand in any of the arguments.

Consequently, the engaging process would be threatened if the therapist exhibited gender bias by focusing on Mrs. Martin's mothering style or questioning the ethnic values behind it. Moreover, forcing Mr. Martin to take a stand in these arguments at this early stage of treatment would be forcing him to do something he had been studiously avoiding and dreaded. These issues may be confronted later in treatment, but in the engagement phase putting them at center stage would threaten the family even more.

**Therapist:**   Before you were married, what did the two of you discuss concerning how you would parent your three children. Is it what you had thought it would be? What has surprised you?

The therapist is opening up the issue of parenting styles. The open-ended questions are designed to put the issue on the table without focusing specifically on one parent or the other.

### Understanding the Family's Life Cycle

The emotional distance between Cindy and her stepmother is respected. Early attempts to reconcile the two of them or suggestions that this would be a goal of treatment would only have served to isolate Cindy:

**Therapist:**   Boy, Cindy, it must be hard remembering the house rules for both your Mom's and Dad's homes. And on top of that, you're probably giving some thought to your own future when you move out of both these homes. How do you manage these things?

Cindy is being invited into the treatment process as an adolescent–young adult. The therapist communicates that her opinions are as valid as anyone else's and that the focus is not merely on "fixing" her.

These three clinical concerns are based first on exploring and understanding the family's paradigm. In doing so, the therapist is not only gathering valuable information on the family's functioning but is also building the therapeutic alliance by listening to the family members and trying to capture what it is like to be "in their shoes." The family members, in turn, feel that the therapist is genuinely trying to understand them and not judging them.

Apart from understanding the individual family members and establishing rapport, the therapist, in the engagement phase, is also establishing the therapeutic boundaries. These boundaries are reinforced throughout treatment.

## Therapeutic Boundaries

Boundaries, as we saw in Chapter 1, refer to demarcation lines within a system that reflect the rules and limits defining interactional patterns: who is responsible for what, who interacts with whom and in what way, who is closer to whom, and so forth. Similar to boundaries within the family, **therapeutic boundaries** define the interactions between the therapist and the family. And just as in a family, the clearer the boundaries, the more defined are the rules of participation. Finally, these boundaries are defined through interaction; they are therapeutic norms that the therapist shapes through interaction.

A key issue in drawing therapeutic boundaries is how much responsibility therapists should take for therapeutic change. On a more personal level the question can be put: "How much responsibility do I take for my clients?" In the process of therapy, who is responsible for change and who should change may become visceral issues.

The fights between Mrs. Martin and Cindy had greatly escalated by the time the first session was held. Cindy was the scapegoat, and Mrs. Martin, in particular, wanted the therapist to "fix" her.

With all parts of the system calling out for help, a therapist would feel compelled to act. First, however, the central question is the responsibility boundary: What family members need to change? Will they take responsibility for the change? How much responsibility will the therapist assume?

**Therapist:**   Mr. and Mrs. Martin, I know Cindy will probably object to my saying so, but I agree with both of you that the situation is going quickly downhill. I also agree that each of you is part of the problem *but also part of the solution.* For me to work individually with Cindy, therefore, would be a waste of time and money. All she would do is try to convince me that both of you are wrong and, at some point, would determine that I was also. Instead, I recommend that all five of you come to the sessions. If this family is to work well, it will need everyone trying to make it better.

The question of who will participate in the sessions and why is the first therapeutic boundary to establish.

**Therapist:**   Also, at some point in the future I will probably want to bring Cindy's mother in for a few sessions. I'm not sure when that might be, but we'll thoroughly discuss it beforehand.

The therapist is introducing the participation of Cindy's mother. Although that may raise the family's anxiety, it is better to introduce the topic in the engagement phase rather than to surprise the family with it later. Concomitantly, the therapist is attempting to reduce any anxiety by acknowledging that the decision will first be thoroughly discussed.

### Establishing the Boundaries with the Family

With the Martin family, the therapist is drawing these boundaries for several reasons. First, from a systems perspective, he has decided that both Mr. and Mrs. Martin and Cindy's mother must assume an active role in treatment. It could be argued that Cindy's behavior is a delayed reaction to the divorce and to her anger at her father's remarriage and, thus, that individual therapy is needed to "rework" these past issues. Still, one could also argue that Cindy is experiencing a sense of displacement because of her position between two families. Consequently, the therapist is emphasizing that blending families is never easy and that for it to work well, everyone must participate.

At first glance these unilateral, therapist-established boundaries may appear to be a gamble on the therapist's part: What if the family rejects the boundaries and terminates treatment? On closer examination, however, the gamble seems to have been minimal. To see Cindy alone would certainly have increased the number of contacts with the family—the parents would keep Cindy coming as long as they believed the therapist was trying to "fix" her—but the lack of change would begin to scream out. Phone calls to the therapist would increase as Cindy continued to act out, and the parents, frustrated with the lack of change, would soon terminate therapy, concluding, "Well, that therapist didn't help!"

The therapist, therefore, has little to lose by drawing the initial boundaries. If the family agrees to the boundaries, the prospects for success increase. If the family rejects the proposed boundaries, the therapist will be in a position to refer it to someone else with no hard feelings or frustration for anyone.

For example, if the Martins were to reject the proposed boundaries, the therapist might say:

> I'm sorry we won't be working together. I respect your judgment concerning your needs at this time. But I also must be clear about how I would approach the problem and why. Only you can decide what would be right for your family. If you'd like, I'd be happy to give you the names of other therapists who might use a different approach.

The Martins, however, accepted the therapist's boundaries—with a reservation. They wanted to exclude Robert and Karen from the sessions: "He doesn't want to come, and she's too young and not involved in all of this." This reservation is frequently voiced in families experiencing difficulties with an older sibling. In these cases the parents are most often motivated by their concern about upsetting a younger child. Some will even say they fear that the older sibling will "contaminate" a younger brother or sister.

Although these fears may be justifiable, they also hint at a family's acceptance of secrets. By excluding information from various members, the family's communication patterns may be facilitating covert alliances—"Now don't tell your father this"—or promoting scapegoating—"Let's talk about him when he's not around." Consequently, if the therapist goes along with the parents' reservation, then dysfunctional family patterns continue.

Again, the therapist is in a position to define the boundaries. With the Martins, Robert's and Karen's participation is seen as essential. Not only are they close in age to Cindy, but they also have experienced many of the same life events as Cindy: the loss of a parent, a single-parent family, the struggle to blend families and accept a stepparent. Moreover, Robert's and Karen's involvement in treatment lessened the scapegoating of Cindy and symbolically stated that Cindy's problems were embedded in the Martins' struggles as a stepfamily.

The responsibility for change and for who should be involved in the treatment illustrates two therapeutic boundaries. Although boundaries vary from case to case, there is one rule of thumb: *The therapist must decide what he or she needs to facilitate change.* Sometimes this is difficult for a beginning family therapist. The desire to keep a family in treatment may outweigh clinical judgment. The therapist may back off an initial boundary for fear that the family will terminate therapy. Bergman (1985) observes that a clinician's fear of losing families keeps a system from changing—the therapist accepts the family's norms and will not challenge them—and that only when the family needs the therapist more than the therapist needs the family is change optimal. Implied in Bergman's observation is an element of timing. Every therapist works well with families who enter therapy on the verge of change or are motivated to change, just as even the most ex-

perienced therapist has difficulty with poorly motivated and highly ambivalent families.

Implied in this discussion is my bias that therapy is a collaborative
effort. The therapist accepts 50% of the responsibility for change while
recognizing that the family must contribute the other 50%. Although this is
a personal belief, research outcome studies strongly support the beneficial
impact of collaborative patient and therapist roles where the crucial factors
are the therapist's encouragement of patients' initiative and the patients'
assumptions of an active role in resolving their problems (Orlinsky &
Howard, 1986). In the end, the family works at maintaining therapeutic
changes long after therapy has terminated.

## Testing Boundaries

To reiterate, therapeutic boundaries are guidelines that the therapist es-
tablishes through interaction with the family that define how therapy will
be conducted. Particularly in the engagement phase of treatment, the family
looks to the therapist to answer "What is this therapy business all about?"
Boundaries help resolve this question. Although some boundaries may be
overtly stated by the therapist, as in the above examples, many more evolve
in the process of therapy. This is a reciprocal process whereby the family
and therapist are shaping each other and, thus, shaping the nature of the
therapeutic alliance.

It is not possible to draw up a list of boundaries applicable to every
family one sees. Each case has unique aspects that call for flexibility on the
therapist's part. Regardless of the boundaries drawn, however, one can rest
assured that they will be tested, to one degree or another, by the family
members. Such testing is not necessarily an indication of opposition to
treatment per se but, rather, is better viewed as the family's attempt to
explore the boundaries and find out where they are drawn. Accordingly, the
active testing of boundaries may be a positive diagnostic sign of the family's
vitality: The family is active in therapy, engaging the therapist and col-
laborating in shaping the treatment process.

The testing of boundaries, therefore, is an essential aspect of the
therapeutic process. It is through this testing that therapeutic norms are
established. The question, however, is how to respond to the testing in ways
that will further therapeutic progress. The following list of common interactions that test the therapist's boundaries is certainly not inclusive, but
it is intended to give a flavor of the process.

### Attendance Issues

As discussed previously, deciding who should attend the sessions is one of
the first therapeutic boundaries established. The idea that the entire family
or at least part of it should come to discuss a member's problems is un-

derstandably foreign to most people. Consequently, an initial challenge to including all family members is to be expected. Even after the therapist has made clear the reasons for this approach, moreover, this boundary is likely to be periodically challenged.

Although the therapist was clear concerning the involvement of Robert and Karen, in one of the early sessions Robert did not show up. The parents offered the excuse that he had a wealth of school responsibilities to finish. Although this was certainly a legitimate excuse, if the therapist failed to at least address the issue, the family might assume that it would be all right for Robert to miss future sessions.

**Therapist:** I'm sorry Robert was unable to attend tonight's session. This must be a busy time of the year for him. But I believe his help with this is essential. Next time, I'd rather reschedule to a more convenient time than have him miss the session.

The therapist acknowledges that sometimes outside commitments need to be attended to but also quietly but firmly emphasizes the initial boundary.

Although not present in the Martin case, a difficult but frequently encountered pattern is the refusal of one of the parents to participate in therapy. Most often it is the father who does not share the mother's concern that a problem even exists. He grudgingly tells his wife, "Do whatever you want to do, but I'm not going!" In these situations the therapist is presented with a dilemma: Do I go ahead and see the mother and children alone, or do I insist on the father coming in?

Several questions are weighed in resolving this dilemma. First, is the mother truly helpless in getting the father in? Does she deny or not see the power she has in persuading him? Second, can the family problem be adequately addressed without the father's involvement, or should his lack of involvement become the central focus, at least in the initial phase of treatment? Lastly, would the father come in if directly contacted by the therapist?

In the worst-case scenario, the mother is truly dominated by the father and fearful of him, he is central to the family's problems, and he refuses the therapist's direct request. At this point another therapeutic choice is at hand. The purist may tell the mother that the father's involvement is absolutely necessary to address the problems adequately and may refuse therapy until the mother gains the father's cooperation. But this stance leaves the mother further defeated and with the same problems. Instead, the following tack can be taken:

**Therapist** [after the father's refusal of involvement]: Well, after talking to your husband I can see and feel what you're up against. I know you came here wanting to get help for your children, and I want to provide that. But it appears to me that the most dominating factor in the family is the relationship you have with your husband. I'd like to talk to you first about that relationship before we discuss what we can do for your children.

Drawing this therapeutic boundary addresses the mother's conflicts, offers assistance with her specific problems, but also focuses the attention on systemic issues.

### Pushing Time Boundaries

One boundary over which the therapist has absolute control is the length of the session. Some therapists plan 90-minute family sessions. Others work on an hourly, 50-minute, or 45-minute basis. The reasons vary from financial (the higher cost of longer sessions) to institutional (the need to document a certain number of cases per week). Suffice it to say, no absolute standard exists. With experience, therapists begin to establish time boundaries that work best for them.

The point, therefore, is to draw time boundaries and consistently maintain them. Although it is idealistic to want to stay working with a family as long as needed, an extra 15 or 30 minutes, it flies in the face of time demands for both the therapist and family members and also presents the family with an unclear boundary: "Last week we met for 90 minutes, and this week the therapist stopped after an hour. What gives?"

How people use time is an interesting discussion in and of itself, but in therapy it has particular meaning. An experienced therapist will talk of the time process of a session. The opening minutes are full of chit-chat as the family members and therapist reaccommodate to one another. Issues are likely to be brought up about a quarter of the way through the session. Finally, there is a need to begin closing the session before time runs out. Most interestingly, emotional bombs—issues not previously raised or reactions not previously expressed—are typically dropped in the last quarter of a session.

In retrospect, there is wisdom in this latter point. Emotionally loaded issues are hard enough to express, much less elaborate on. Consequently, by raising agendas at the end of a session, the family member is introducing a new topic to the therapist but is also signaling that this is a highly charged issue to be addressed later. Practically and protectively, the end of the session leaves little time for elaboration but has established an agenda for the next meeting and alerted the therapist to a threatening issue.

Clarity and consistency of time boundaries add a predictability to the treatment sessions for both the therapist and the family. It is, however, a boundary that is initially stated by the therapist—"Each session lasts 60 minutes"—and established as a norm through interaction.

Testing this boundary occurs in several ways. The family may be late for the meeting and still expect it to run the full time. Emotional issues are brought up right at the end of the session, and the therapist is begged to continue. Family members may linger in the office hoping to speak to the therapist alone. Or family members may concretely ask for more time. Each of these requests may seduce the therapist into extending the session and thus blurring the time boundaries.

### Telephone Calls

The telephone is frequently used in making alliances. Family members will call with information they "didn't want to bring up in the last session but thought you should know." Consciously or unconsciously the family member in these situations is seeking an alliance with the therapist, frequently against another family member.

It is most important that the therapist establish a boundary on information outside of the sessions. If the family members believe or know they can call the therapist between sessions to discuss other family members, this will rapidly happen.

As always, one can announce this boundary in the early phase of treatment by saying:

**Therapist:**   I believe very strongly that what all of you have to say to one another is most important. Consequently, our sessions are the time to raise the issues each of you feels are important. If you have something to say to me, please do so in our sessions.

But even with this announcement an inevitable test does occur. Sometimes, within the first few sessions, one family member will call with information he or she believes can be said only to the therapist. Not only is this behavior diagnostic—it hints at the use of secrets in the family—but more importantly, how the therapist handles the phone call will set the tone for the treatment.

A simple but effective response over the phone is:

**Therapist:**   Before you begin, please know that whatever you tell me, I'll assume I can bring it up in our next family session. With this in mind, I'd be happy to hear whatever you have to say.

The caller then usually expresses the need for secrecy and again appeals to the therapist, who then responds:

**Therapist:**   I understand your concern that what you're about to say can't be said in the family session, but I've found openness to be the best approach with families. Consequently, you'll be the best judge of whether to raise your issues at our meetings. I hope you will, but I'll respect your decision if you don't. Hopefully, our meetings will reach the point where you'll raise your concerns.

The above are just a few examples of boundaries that are tested in the course of treatment. Again, the basic question the therapist asks is "What do I need to do my job?" All boundaries flow from the answers to this question.

## Therapist's Use of Self

The **therapist's use of self** refers to the ways in which the practitioner employs all aspects of his or her personality to further the treatment process. Some questions relevant to this discussion are: "How much do I share about myself? How do I handle family members' personal questions of me? What does my own behavior communicate to the family? Should I reveal my strong personal reactions to what is occurring in treatment?"

Although falling under the rubric of therapeutic boundaries, the use of self is directly defined by one's theoretical model but also reflects one's comfort level and personal style. One therapist may feel quite comfortable answering the family's personal questions, whereas another therapist's anxiety may be raised. To further this discussion, the therapist's use of self is subdivided into issues of self-disclosure and the use of personal reactions. As always, there are no universally accepted answers. With experience, therapists discover their own personal comfort level.

### Therapist's Self-Disclosure

How much do I share with the family? How do I answer the family's personal questions? Where do I draw the boundary on the family's personal questions?

Some families may ask a series of personal questions of the therapist: "Are you married? Have you ever been divorced? Do you have children?" These questions may range from a legitimate request for information to defensive challenges: "Have you and your wife ever had marital problems?"

In the engagement phase of treatment the family is evaluating the therapist as much as the therapist is evaluating the family. The family members may need additional information from the therapist to determine whether he or she is the one with whom they wish to work. To address this need and to clear the deck for the family-focused therapeutic work, the therapist offers in the first session to answer any questions the family members may have:

**Therapist:**   To help you determine if I'm the right therapist for the family, are there any personal questions you wish to ask me?

By opening up the initial session for personal self-disclosure, the therapist not only addresses the family's concerns but also displays openness and honesty and symbolically communicates that therapy will be a collaborative effort.

Typically, the family members will ask, if they ask at all, basic questions concerning academic degrees, marital status, number of children, and the like. What is frequently more important than the answers to these questions is the manner in which the therapist responds. Is the therapist defensive or guarded? Is he or she open and honest?

Paradoxically, the more open the therapist appears, the less need the family has for questions. The family members are assured through the therapist's behavior that he or she will be responsive to them.

Finally, whereas family members' personal questions of the therapist in the initial interview or the engagement phase of treatment may represent legitimate requests for information, in the latter stages of treatment 99% of the time they are resistant and defensive maneuvers. This typically occurs when a heated family issue is surfacing, the family is at an impasse, or the therapist is pushing into sensitive issues and the family is attempting to escape the spotlight. At these times turning the question back to the process furthers treatment and not resistance:

**Mr. Martin**  [in a later phase of treatment and in the middle of a heated discussion]: Have you ever had problems like this with your own wife?

**Therapist:**  Well, that's something for me to think about, but I think it's irrelevant to what just occurred. I think you and Donna have locked horns on this issue, and there doesn't appear to be any way out.

The therapist is drawing the therapeutic boundary and redirecting the discussion back to the issue at hand.

### Use of Personal Reactions

Experiential family therapists would argue that the heart of the therapeutic process is the therapist's use of self, or, more concretely, the therapist's use of personal reactions (Whitaker & Bumberry, 1988). Whatever the therapist's reactions are to the family process—anger, frustration, sadness, joy—it is reasonable to assume that other family members may be experiencing similar feelings, even if they do not articulate them. Consequently, sharing personal reactions may strike responsive therapeutic cords in the family members and faster change. The choices, therefore, are if, when, and how to use these reactions.

As a rule of thumb the therapist's sharing of personal reactions can be most beneficial when (1) the treatment process has reached an impasse, (2) the family asks for feedback, (3) the therapist assumes a defensive position, and (4) therapy is about to end.

At various times throughout the treatment process, impasses develop. Impasses may signal any number of themes: The family is avoiding a difficult issue, the family is struggling with an issue that precedes a positive breakthrough, the family members do not feel understood by the therapist, or the therapist has missed an important ingredient in the family's dynamics. However, regardless of the interpretation of the impasse, on the very concrete, experiential level, an impasse may leave all participants, the therapist included, feeling discouraged. The therapist's direct confrontation of the impasse may foster its resolution, particularly when the task is addressed as a cooperative effort:

**Therapist:**    I may be wrong, but does anyone else feel as stuck as I do? I feel as if we've gone around this mulberry bush one too many times. Anybody have any ideas about how to get through this?

A variation on the theme of impasse is a family's request for direct feedback. Typically, this request is made in the middle phases of treatment, and although possessing a strong defensive element—the family members are shifting the focus away from themselves and onto the therapist—it is also a request for feedback!

**Mrs. Martin**    [after several disagreements with her husband over establishing consistent expectations for Cindy]: I don't think we'll ever reach an agreement on this. The two of us come from such different backgrounds. Do you [therapist] see any point in all of this?

**Therapist:**    You may be right about you and Peter never developing boundaries with Cindy and consistently reinforcing them. However, for better or for worse, you're both parents to your children and will be for years to come. It's your decision what kind of parents you'll be.

The therapist is refocusing the discussion back to problematic issues.

In the course of treatment, the therapist is also responding to the therapeutic process. Individual personalities of the family members, content or process themes, and specific behavioral patterns all act as stimuli for both conscious and unconscious reactions within the therapist. At any point the therapist may assume a defensive position by not fully listening to the family, or daydreaming. This is not a flaw but a human response. The issue, therefore, is how to use this reaction to promote change.

For example, Mrs. Martin is the first to bring up Cindy's misdeeds since the previous session. Mr. Martin looks perplexed and frustrated. Cindy is always good for overt or passive-aggressive hostility. Confronted with the power and persistence of these patterns, the therapist could become as frustrated and annoyed as the family members.

Concretely, frustration and annoyance portray themselves in the inability of the therapist to listen. Therapists may find themselves listening less and less to the individual family members. If this pattern is allowed to continue, therapists become part of the problem. From another perspective, this annoyance and inattention are valuable feedback to a therapist:

**Therapist**    [to Mrs. Martin after she has related another incident of Cindy's disobedience]: Mrs. Martin, I know that Cindy's behavior is intolerable to you and that she continues to violate your wishes. But in each session we've had you bring up one violation after another. I have a feeling you're sending me or your husband a strong message, but I'm not clear what it is. Tell us directly why you focus on these events.

The therapist is moving past Mrs. Martin's complaints to have her articulate more directly the message behind the complaints. Is she trying to say how frustrated she is? Whom does she want to hear that message? How does she want the person to respond to her?

**Therapist:** Mr. Martin, I was wondering—when your wife brings up her concerns about Cindy, you look to me as if you'd love to leave the room. Am I right or wrong in that impression? What do you want to say to your wife at those moments?

Mr. Martin's perplexed look is frequently a cue for the therapist to answer the wife's concerns. If the therapist responds in this manner, the parents can avoid dealing directly with each other, and the therapist has inadvertently taken over Mr. Martin's role. The quoted response above draws Mr. Martin back into the discussion in his proper role.

**Therapist** [after Cindy interrupts the discussion with a hostile comment]: Cindy, you have an amazing sense of timing. Not only do you choose to interrupt your parents and myself just at a point where we might solve something; you also have the capacity to make the blood vessels stand out in our necks. I must say, you're good at it, because I've felt it in my own neck more than once. But I have a feeling there's something else you're trying to say. Do you want them to be at odds with each other? Are you trying to tell us that you're hurt and angry too?

Here the therapist is not only addressing Cindy's hostile comments but also diffusing the impact of the hostility and suggesting that she has feelings she would like others to understand.

As shown by these examples, the therapist's use of personal reactions can be a powerful diagnostic tool—what troubles the therapist may also bother the family members—and an intervention technique—a personal and direct statement. Used as an intervention tool, however, it may harm as much as it helps. The question is one of intent: Is the therapist's use of personal reactions serving the needs of the family or the needs of the therapist (an acting-out of the therapist's own hostility and frustration)? As Shapiro (1981) points out, there is a thin line between the use of self to facilitate therapeutic process and the use of self to meet the therapist's needs.

For example, depending on the therapist's predilections, any one or all of the family members could be confronted:

**Therapist:** Mrs. Martin, your complaints fall on deaf ears. I wonder why you persistently bring them up?

**Therapist:** Mr. Martin, you play dumb like a fox. Why do you leave your wife out on a limb like this?

**Therapist:** Cindy, you have a one-note act. All you can do is interrupt in a hostile fashion.

Taken out of context, the above confrontations are neither bad nor good. If they are timed properly and if the recipient is ready to "hear" the message, they could be surprisingly effective. On the other hand, if the therapist believes that the confrontations are justified "because the person needs to hear what I have to say," an observer must wonder about the therapist's motivation. *Overall, the question is whether the therapeutic process will be facilitated by the therapist's use of self or inhibited.*

Moreover, no therapist is immune to an abusive use of self. Family therapy, in particular, takes place in a highly emotionally charged atmosphere. It should be remembered that therapy touches the therapist as much as it touches the family. Family-of-origin and nuclear-family issues may be stirred up, with each family seemingly tapping another aspect of the therapist's emotional life: "Someone reminds me of one of my parents. This theme existed in my own family. I've always had difficulty with this type of person. I'm always rushing to save someone."

Empathy, an invaluable tool of the clinician, is born of this self-awareness. Personal thoughts, feelings, and memories remind us that we too may have felt similar things; that we too have been stuck in our own self-made box, unable to get out; that we too have felt emotions that we cannot put into words.

It is not, therefore, the thoughts and feelings stimulated by the therapist's interaction with the family that inhibit or facilitate therapeutic progress. Thoughts and feelings will come and go throughout the treatment process. Rather, how the therapist "uses" them will either facilitate or hinder the therapeutic alliance.

## Summary

As a means of summarizing the engagement process, Table 3.1 highlights the clinical concerns at Phase I.

---

### *Table 3.1*   *Engagement Questions*

#### *Therapeutic Alliance*

**Ethnicity**
1. What ethnic patterns are operating within the family?
2. How do these patterns reflect the family's paradigm?
3. Do the ethnic patterns shape the family's defined problems?
4. How similar to or different from the family's ethnicity is the therapist's?
5. What potential problems in engaging the family arise because of these differences or similarities?

## Table 3.1    Engagement Questions

### Family Life Cycle
1. What is the family's life cycle stage?
2. Is the family experiencing difficulties in this stage?
3. Have earlier stages been successfully negotiated? Are past unresolved issues being carried into the present stage?
4. How does the therapist's own life cycle stage compare with the family's? Are there potential problems in engaging the family because of the differences or similarities?

### Gender Bias
1. What gender biases exist in the family?
2. Do these biases reflect ethnic patterns or idiosyncratic family-of-origin patterns?
3. What are the therapist's gender biases?
4. Are there gender patterns within the family that may bias the therapist and make this family difficult to work with?

### Therapist's Family of Origin
1. What themes from the therapist's family of origin may affect the treatment process?
2. What strengths and vulnerabilities does the therapist bring to the treatment process?
3. What themes in the family are familiar or foreign to the therapist?
4. What family themes provoke an emotional reaction in the therapist? Can these reactions be channeled positively into the treatment process, or will they interfere?

### Treatment Notes

### Therapeutic Boundaries
1. What boundaries are important to draw with the family?
2. Which therapeutic boundaries are nonnegotiable with the family (boundaries the therapist deems essential for treatment), and which ones are more flexible?
3. How will the family test these boundaries?
4. What will the therapist's response be?

### Therapist's Use of Self
1. How much do I share with the family?
2. How will I respond to personal questions?
3. What emotions of mine are frequently evoked while I'm working with this family?
4. Will sharing my reactions facilitate or inhibit the treatment process? When should I share them?

# *Glossary*

**Constructivism**  The view that an organism is never able to recognize or depict reality but can construct a model (paradigm) to represent reality.

**Ethnicity**  A sense of cultural commonality (for example, norms, values) transmitted over generations by the family and reinforced by the surrounding community.

**Family life cycle**  A developmental concept referring to a family's evolution over time; transitional phases and crises are seen as inevitable when there are entries into and exits from the family.

**Family paradigm**  A family's construct of the social world that guides members' thoughts, feelings, and actions.

**Gender biases**  Overt or covert prejudices that support traditional views of male-female relationships; feminist theorists highlight the inequality of traditional sex roles and how these biases may be reinforced in therapy to the detriment of women.

**Therapeutic alliance**  A new system formed by the therapist and family to facilitate the treatment process; reflects a basic level of trust and a shared agenda.

**Therapeutic boundaries**  Demarcations that define the interactions between the therapist and family; mutually constructed.

**Therapist's use of self**  The ways in which the clinician employs all aspects of his or her personality to further the treatment process.

# Engagement Phase II: Identifying Dysfunctional Patterns

**A Family's Expressive Style**
**Genograms**
**The Interview Process**
**Case Presentation**
**Treatment Notes**
**Summary**

Powerful human themes are at the heart of family life: love, acceptance, rejection, hate, compassion, sacrifice, cruelty. To approach the family from a systems perspective, however, it may be helpful to think of a <u>family first</u> as a social group. Having worked in groups, led groups, and participated in groups, therapists become familiar with the issues that frequently emerge: leadership, status hierarchy, power channels, supportive behaviors, task behavior, communication patterns. Above all else, one is struck by how groups evolve a predictability to their interactions.

Formal groups, for instance, establish overt patterns through bureaucratic procedures and policy. Even a small group meeting may follow Robert's Rules of Order. Whereas some groups develop clear, consistent interactive rules to the point at which the parts (people) are replaceable and the group will continue to operate smoothly, other groups have far looser boundaries and emphasize an egalitarian milieu. These groups' interactive patterns are less procedural and more determined by the personalities of the group members; self-help groups are an example.

Applied to family therapy, each family evolves its own predictable patterns **(norms)**. For instance, can you predict the sequence of events at your next family get-together? Who will talk to whom? Who will correct whom? Who will tell the jokes? Who will listen the best? Who will talk the most? Who will be the most problematic? How will this person be "managed" by the group? Overall, is there a consistent pattern to these family gatherings?

Just as all family groups evolve norms of interaction, some are more functional than others. For example, some people welcome holidays as a time to reconnect with family members and receive nurturing and support; others dread the thought of family gatherings because of what they know (predict?) will occur. As one person put it, "Getting my family together is sure to give everyone heartburn."

Of course, what is functional for one family member may be dysfunctional for another. A parent may want the children to do exactly as they are told as a sign of respect. An older adolescent, however, bristles at this lack of autonomy imposed by the parent and rebels through passive-aggressive behavior.

Besides building a therapeutic alliance, therefore, the beginning phase of treatment is concerned with understanding and identifying family patterns. Treatment and intervention strategies evolve from this firm grasp of the family dynamics. As a means of discerning these patterns, a therapist is continually forming hypotheses and testing them out. These working hypotheses serve to guide the therapist's questions. For example, it was initially hypothesized that one factor fueling the arguments between Mrs. Martin and Cindy was Mr. Martin's inconsistent support of one against the other. The therapist's questions, therefore, tested the hypothesis:

**Therapist:**   I'm a little confused about something. Mrs. Martin, how do you get support from your husband when these arguments erupt. Cindy, how do you get support?

If both Mrs. Martin and Cindy responded that Mr. Martin always supported his wife, the hypothesis would be discarded in favor of a new one—Cindy was angry because she believed her father had chosen his new wife over her:

**Therapist:**   Cindy, in the middle of these arguments when your father steps in to support your stepmother, how do you react? What do you feel like?

Or if the original hypothesis was confirmed, the therapist would then explore Mr. Martin's thoughts and motivation:

**Therapist:**   Mr. Martin, both your wife and daughter appear confused about when you'll support one or the other. Would you tell me how you decide what to do?

As we can see, identifying patterns is a process of forming working hypotheses, testing them out via questions, and either confirming them or discarding them. Whichever the case, the therapist is led to further hypotheses.

To formalize and clarify the process of identifying family patterns, the chapter first addresses common expressive styles encountered in therapy, the use of genograms as a means of symbolically representing the patterns, and the use of different types of questions in the therapy sessions to guide one's hypotheses. These discussions are followed by case material and treatment notes.

# A Family's Expressive Style

Initially, one readily apparent pattern is the family's expressive style. Some families are open and directly answer the therapist's questions. Others are guarded and volunteer little information. Still others regularly explode in anger, and some families sit in depressed silence. One way of conceptualizing this distinction is to imagine an emotionally expressive dimension ranging from retentive silences at one end to explosive outbursts at the other. Silences beg for the therapist to fill the void, and arguments draw the therapist into the role of chief negotiator. Not only do these two poles challenge one's engagement skills, but the therapeutic task is to work within these styles in hopes of understanding the dysfunctional patterns. Because silent and argumentative families are particularly difficult for beginning therapists and fill much of a clinician's caseload, they are highlighted below.

## Silent Families

At one extreme, silent families present their distinct challenge to the therapist. Does the silence hint at a coiled spring of resentment and anger waiting for release? Or does it reflect a depression and resignation that dominate the family's mood? With these two possibilities, a therapist may feel as if he or she is entering a minefield: "Will I stumble onto an explosion?" Although one can speculate on the dynamics behind the silence, it remains for the therapist to address the style and facilitate the uncovering of family patterns.

 First, the silence is telling in and of itself. Instead of the family members actively engaging the therapist and defining their problem, they sit in relative silence. Adults will answer with brief responses; adolescents will blankly stare and say, "I don't know"; and younger children will giggle or shift uncomfortably in their chairs, anxiously looking toward one of the parents. In these situations, the initial hypotheses are:

1. The family is waiting for its spokesperson to lead.
2. Blame dominates the family, and members are sitting anxiously waiting for the accusations to begin.
3. The family's anger is barely contained, and the silence masks repressed rage.
4. The family was coerced into coming and resents being there.

As a means of addressing this silence, three methods may be helpful: allowing the spokesperson to emerge, attempting to draw in other members, and acknowledging silence during the engagement phase and inviting participation.

### 1. Allowing the Spokesperson to Emerge

In the first session, after defining the purpose of the meeting (see Chapter 3) and asking why the family decided to make the appointment, the therapist sits back and waits for the initial patterns to emerge. In meeting silence with silence, the therapist nonverbally communicates that therapy will be a 50-50 enterprise and that nothing will be accomplished without the family's cooperation.

As the silence and accompanying anxiety in the session grow, the family will move to fill the vacuum. The first to speak is the family's spokesperson. This person may or may not be the dominant parent. He or she is, however, the one parent who does most of the liaison between the family and authority figures (teachers, minister, therapist). A key observation to make is whether the spokesperson continually glances toward the other parent and how that parent nonverbally responds. For example, a mother when speaking of the difficulty she is having with one of her children continually shifts her focus between the therapist and her husband. The husband, in turn, either nods or stares evenly at his wife. In this situation a significant family pattern is being revealed: The father is the dominant parent, and the mother operates within his sphere of control.

In contrast, take the same initial behavior—the mother discussing her children's problems—but in this case she stares directly at the therapist the entire time. (She has the power to define the problems in the family.) Furthermore, she not only does not acknowledge her husband but implies that he is part of the problem: "My son does nothing around the house, and his *father* just *sits* there!"

### 2. Attempting to Draw in Other Members

Having listened to the spokesperson—but being careful not to let this parent dominate the entire session—the therapist turns to other family members to ask their impressions by either building on what the spokesperson has said—"Billy, your Mom says you help very little around the house; I wonder if you see it the same way"—or moving back to the broader question—"Well, your mother has her point of view of why the family came in today, and I'd like to hear what each of your own points of view are."

### 3. Acknowledging Silence and Inviting Participation

In the early sessions, particularly in the first session, attempting to draw out other family members may be less than successful. Here, it is important to remind oneself that this failure has less to do with one's clinical skill than with the recognition that one is entering a powerfully retentive, repressed, and controlled system. In fact, silence is an ultimate form of control: "You can't make me talk."

Family therapists first cut their teeth on this issue when dealing with passive-aggressive adolescents. In comes the family, and right away the adolescent makes for the corner, slouches in a chair, and stares at the floor. Again, the behavior speaks volumes and leads to many working hypotheses: What is adaptive in this young person's style? Why, in this family, does the teenager need to pull away in silence? What is he or she protesting?

Besides the hypotheses they create, silences may be respected but also acknowledged. Regarding the Martins, Cindy would at times lapse into silence:

**Therapist:**    Cindy, it appears that you've decided not to talk today. I respect your choice, because there must be strong reasons for your decision. At any time, if you feel like jumping in, I'd appreciate your help in figuring this out.

Notice that the therapist has redefined Cindy's uncooperative behavior as a form of decision making over which she has control. Furthermore, eliminating the threat that she will be made to talk opens the door for Cindy to *decide* to participate, on her own terms.

To sum up, silence in the engagement phase is accepted and not challenged. In doing so, the therapist communicates a respect for the family's style. As therapy progresses, however, silence takes on a much different, more defensive posture and calls for alternative responses from the therapist. (This topic is addressed in the next chapter, under resistance.)

## Argumentative Families

At the other end of the spectrum are the families ready to do battle. These families' arguments can begin in the waiting room. More often than not the family members have their clear villains: It is always the other person! When the tension can be felt as the family enters the office, it takes nothing more than "So how did things go this week?" to touch off the broadside exchange.

From the family members' perspective, they know that their problems are due to other people, and their arguments are demonstrations to the therapist of the correctness of their views. For the therapist, there is a hint of fleeting terror as the session seems completely out of control. The anger is palpable, and a therapist typically enters the fray in an attempt to negotiate a truce. More often than not, the negotiations fail to work because the therapist has missed the point: The family members are trying to demonstrate who is wrong and find out whose side the therapist is on, not to seek a solution.

Rather than negotiating, the therapist has alternative responses—

maintaining neutrality, letting the anger run its course until the family's patterns emerge, intervening by moving from the emotional to the cognitive, and, above all, avoiding being caught up in the drama.

## 1. Maintaining Neutrality

Initially, the family members are presenting their cases to the therapist, assuming that he or she will be as judgmental as they are. Consequently, there is nothing new in their behavior, at least from their perspectives. In fact, that is the very nature of the problem: Their patterns consistently lead to accusations and polarization, with their anger as a by-product of these dysfunctional patterns.

This is not said to minimize the family's suffering. There is a tremendous amount of pain, which members are continually inflicting on one another. Rather, the point is that nothing new is occurring in the therapist's office and that the family has been existing at this level of anger for quite some time. To attempt to rescue the family from these arguments is the therapist's wish, not the family's. At this early phase of treatment, who is right or wrong is the family's foremost issue.

Furthermore, the therapist has not stirred up these conflicts with questions—again, they probably began in the waiting room or on the ride to the office—and will not be able to change them in one or two sessions. As a result, rather than feeling out of control, the therapist should welcome the opportunity to witness the family's fighting style and, in the process, observe the patterns.

## 2. Letting the Anger Run Its Course Until Patterns Emerge

By not rushing in to put out the fires, the therapist allows patterns to evolve. Who accuses whom of what? How does that person respond? How do other family members react to this dyadic exchange? What underlies this exchange: hurt, jealousy, control? When and how do the other family members become involved in this conflict?

Once the initial patterns have been acted out, the therapist intervenes to block the patterns from escalating and dominating the session. Usually in the first half hour, the family has revealed many of its basic patterns. If the therapist is passive throughout the entire session, the risk is that the patterns will continue to recycle in a downward spiral, resulting in increased anger and frustration. In these situations, the family members understandably leave the session thinking: "What do we need the therapist for. We do this at home by ourselves."

Consequently, a therapeutic intervention is required, but it is a question of timing: allowing the family members to portray their patterns but at the same time intervening before the session becomes counterproductive.

### 3. Intervening by Moving from the Emotional to the Cognitive

In an emotionally charged atmosphere, simply asking someone to perform a learned behavior—for example, "Blow your nose"—interrupts the firecracker chain of dysfunctional patterns. In an emotionally charged family interview, moving away from exchanges between members to dyadic exchanges with the therapist and moving the content of the discussion from emotionally laden issues to more cognitive ones defuses the situation.

For example, after the patterns have been initially demonstrated, the therapist enters the discussion by engaging the family members one-on-one:

**Therapist:**  Mrs. Martin, I know you've been trying to get a message through to your daughter, but I'm confused about what it is. Would you tell it to me?

**Therapist:**  Cindy, it looked to me as if when your stepmother said certain things, they really bothered you. Am I right? What were some of those things?

**Therapist:**  Mr. Martin, at first you were listening to your wife and daughter, but at some point you entered the discussion. What did they say to bring you in? What were you hoping to accomplish when you entered?

Moving the discussion from the emotionally laden to more cognitive issues, the therapist asks:

"Is this what happens at home?"
"How often do these fights occur?"
"Do the same issues start the same fights?"
"What brings you each into the arguments?"

Such questions force the family members to disengage from the emotional argument, reflect on what is occurring, and interact in a problem-solving mode with the therapist.

With these questions, the therapist begins to assume control of the session and provides the family members with a simple, but powerful, therapeutic experience: They can all be in the same room together discussing their problems without constant explosions. Moreover, by engaging members one-on-one, the therapist subtly, without requiring it, induces the members to *listen* to one another. They are in the same room together, and unless they put cotton in their ears, they are bound to hear something of what another family member is saying.

When engaging individual family members, it is extremely important *not to permit the discussion to turn into a gripe session about a third party.* The therapist has already heard those complaints in the first half hour. Rather, the therapist is asking an individual family member to talk about his or her personal frustrations, hurts, beliefs, and attempts to remedy the family problems:

**Therapist:**  Mrs. Martin, I'm quite clear about your concerns for Cindy, but I'm worried about what these continual fights do to you.

**Therapist:**   Cindy, your anger at your stepmother is clear to me, but it must be hard on you to be continually angry.

**Therapist:**   Mr. Martin, it looks as if you try to put an end to the fights between your wife and daughter, but to no avail. What is this like for you?

As a note of caution, some families will actively resist the therapist assuming control of the exchanges, particularly when he or she attempts to diffuse the exchanges by establishing one-on-one relationships. Here, the family members are not only demonstrating the power and compulsions of their conflicts but also testing the therapist: "Will you be strong enough to manage us? Our conflicts feel overwhelming to us; will they overwhelm you?"

These situations call for a clear message to be sent that the therapist is in charge. Sometimes it requires only a simple: "Please Cindy, I know you have a point of view and I'd be happy to listen to it, but right now I'm talking to your mother, so please don't interrupt." At other times, however, a forceful stand is required: "Look, for these sessions to accomplish anything, people need to be able to complete what they have to say, and I need to listen to what they're saying. Whether the rest of you want to listen or not, that's your choice, but I do."

### 4. Avoiding an Emotional Trap

Family patterns possess a powerful whirlpool effect, which can sweep a therapist up in their currents. The trap is becoming emotionally bogged down in the family drama.

Clinicians, in these cases, may find themselves agreeing that the scapegoat is the family problem, believing that someone does need to be rescued, or taking sides in the conflict and, in the process, falling into a lineal definition of the problem. When any of these occur, it is an indication that the family dynamics are powerful enough to skew the therapist's perceptions.

As discussed in the previous chapter, the therapist uses these personal reactions to understand the system. In taking a step back, the therapist may find these emotional pulls to be quite diagnostic: "Why do I feel like rescuing Cindy? Why do I feel the need to support Mrs. Martin? Why am I angry at Mr. Martin's ambivalence?" Answering these questions helps put the family patterns into clearer perspective and, equally important, alerts the therapist to the personal pitfalls in working with the family.

As a matter of course, specific emotional pulls will occur again and again throughout the sessions. As a rule of thumb, when a therapist begins to shift to a lineal definition of the family's problems, it is a clear sign that the family's definition of the problem is dominating and that the therapist is risking becoming as lost and as stuck as the family in attempting to implement change.

# Genograms

A **genogram** is a format for drawing a family tree over at least three generations (McGoldrick & Gerson, 1985). But much more than a family tree, a
genogram graphically portrays complex family patterns across several generations and places the problem behavior in a larger family systems context.
With its origins in Bowen's family systems theory (Bowen, 1978; Guerin &
Pendagast, 1976), the use of the genogram is accepted practice for many
family therapists.

Genograms are co-constructed with the family members in the engagement phase of treatment. The therapist is not only gathering valuable
biographical data but also engaging the family in a collaborative therapeutic
effort. Moreover, the genogram offers a means of broadening the family's
focus. For example, in the course of constructing the Martins' genogram,
Cindy's place in the broader system became graphically clear: She was
between two separate families.

Briefly, creating a genogram involves three levels: (1) mapping the
family structure, (2) recording family information, and (3) delineating family
relationships (McGoldrick & Gerson, 1985). We will now develop a genogram for the Martins, moving through each of the three levels.

In mapping the family structure, the therapist delineates the basic
family relationships. Figure 4.1 presents the Martins' three-generational
tree.

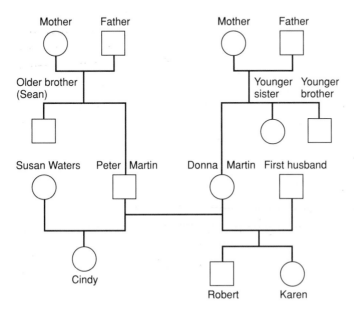

**Figure 4.1** *Three-Generational Tree of the Martin Family*

Recording family information involves demographic data and critical family events. Demographic information includes ages, dates of birth and death, geographic locations, occupations, educational levels, and the like. Figure 4.2 adds the muscle to the family skeleton mapped in Figure 4.1.

The genogram in Figure 4.2 expands our view of the Martin family:

- Mrs. Martin is the oldest of three siblings (having a younger sister and brother). Both her parents are still living and reside in the same town. Mrs. Martin's first husband died five years before her second marriage.
- Mr. Martin is the younger of two brothers. Both his parents died in the previous ten years.

Besides the basic information contained in Figure 4.2, much more information can be added. For example, each family member can be asked to use adjectives to describe the other family members. In the process, not only is each person more fully described, but conflicting views are also quickly revealed. For example, Mr. Martin described his older brother (Sean) as distant and uninvolved. Mrs. Martin, however, pointed out that Peter and Sean had had several arguments over the years revolving around Sean's alcoholism. Sean, she related, was divorced twice, and alcohol played a strong role each time. Mr. Martin admitted that he and Sean rarely saw eye to eye on many things.

The most inferential level of genogram construction is delineating the relationships among family members. This involves a combination of fami-

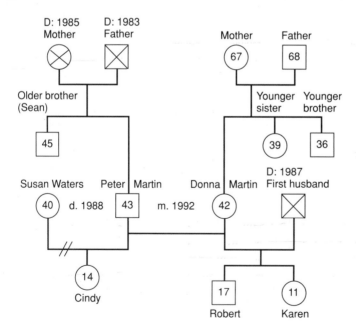

**Figure 4.2** Demographic Three-Generational Tree of the Martin Family

ly members' self-reports and clinical observations. For example, Mr. Martin described his relationship with his brother as distant, but as he spoke it became clear that it was highly conflictual and caused him much pain. His denial of the pain then became a working hypothesis to test later in treatment.

Figure 4.3 illustrates the relationships based on the members' self-reports and the therapist's observations. From this genogram, many working hypotheses begin to emerge:

1. The central triangular relationship in the family conflict involves Mr. and Mrs. Martin and Cindy. This conflict is what brought the family into treatment and will need to be addressed first.
2. The next central triangle involves Mr. Martin, Cindy, and Cindy's mother (Susan Waters). As the only child, Cindy has moved back and forth between her parents during their separation, divorce, and post-divorce periods. These relationships may have shifting alliances that change rapidly. Cindy's behavior, therefore, could be a consequence of these circular interactions.
3. One is left to speculate on the possible triangles among Susan Waters, Mrs. Martin, Mr. Martin, and Cindy. Do Cindy's biological parents cooperate in raising her? What has their postdivorce relationship been like? What does Mrs. Martin think of her husband's ex-wife? And so on.
4. Mr. Martin's conflicted relationship with his brother remains to be

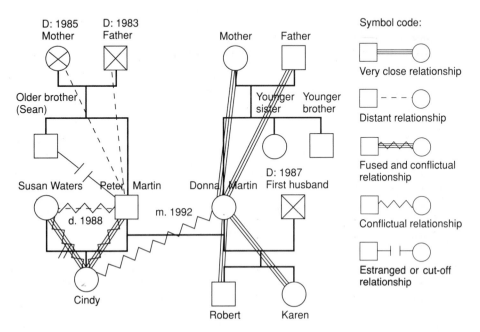

**Figure 4.3** *Three-Generational Tree Relationships of the Martin Family*

explored. How has this relationship affected him? Does Cindy know her uncle? Does Mr. Martin fear that Cindy may be like her uncle?

5. Although not directly explored, one wonders about the marital patterns: When asked, both Mr. and Mrs. Martin described their relationship as "fine" but said they were experiencing significant stress in parenting Cindy. Still, they appeared guarded in their responses.

6. The triangle involving Mr. Martin, Mrs. Martin, and her parents is an area to question. How has Mr. Martin been received by his wife's parents? Is he comfortable with the degree of closeness to them? Does he mind or support his wife's involvement with her parents?

7. Finally, what is the quality of the relationship among Mr. Martin, Robert, and Karen. What role does Mr. Martin take in his stepchildren's lives? What role does Mrs. Martin want him to take?

In summary, besides the wonderful shorthand in describing complex family relationships, a genogram provides a practical, nonthreatening way of engaging the whole family (McGoldrick & Gerson, 1985). Because the task of constructing a genogram is one step removed from the threatening issues that brought the family into treatment, the members' anxiety is decreased, fostering a therapeutic alliance. As each family member begins to express his or her point of view regarding the various other members, differences are highlighted in a similarly nontoxic way. In conclusion, the graphic portrayal of the family system is a picture worth a thousand words to both the therapist and family. The black-and-white diagram offers a means of viewing family patterns and places the problematic behavior within a broader systems context in which all members influence one another.

## The Interview Process

Besides observing, the therapist, through verbal and nonverbal behavior, is facilitating the interaction and uncovering the family patterns. Focusing on the therapist's verbal behavior, one sees a balance being struck between questions and statements. Statements set forth positions or views, whereas questions call forth positions or views. The balance between the two varies with different schools of therapy (Tomm, 1988). For example, the Milan systemic approach relies heavily on questions—clinical hypotheses openly shared with the family—whereas the structural and strategic approaches emphasize statements defining the therapist's view of the family's problem and directions for the family to follow. A therapist using the Milan model may speculate with the Martins:

**Therapist:**   Cindy, do you wonder if your father favors you or your stepmother?

The therapist is questioning whether Cindy is in competition with her stepmother. The question invites her to comment. However, though it is nonthreatening, posing the question in this way also invites a simple no that closes the discussion.

A structural-strategic therapist may say:

**Therapist:**   Mr. Martin, I believe your daughter is trying to figure out where you stand. These arguments are a test to determine whose side you're on, because Cindy is trying to determine whether you still love her.

In stating this opinion, the therapist is challenging the family. If Mr. Martin agrees with the statement, the therapist builds on this agreement. If Mr. Martin or Cindy disagrees with the statement, he or she must then defend that opposition. However, although certainly challenging the system, the therapist is also running the risk of increasing a family's defensiveness.

## Types of Questions

In a series of articles, Tomm (1987a, 1987b, 1988) examines the process of family interviewing and makes several points apropos of assessment and engagement issues. Specifically, focusing on therapeutic questions, he defines four major types of questions: lineal and circular questions (which serve to orient the therapist to the family members' perspectives, a process essential to both engagement and assessment) and strategic and reflexive questions (which serve to influence therapeutic change).

### Lineal Questions

The first type, **lineal questions,** is investigative in nature and assumes a linear cause and effect:

"Why did all of you decide to make this appointment?"
"What problems does Cindy have, Mrs. Martin?"
"How long have these problems persisted?"
"What have you tried to do to change the problem?"
"What has worked; what hasn't worked?"
"Cindy, what's making you so angry?"

Lineal questions focus on identifying a problem in the family: Who has it? What has been done about it? How often does it occur? And so forth. Moreover, they serve to *orient* the therapist to the family members' views of their problem.

Typically, the family expects such questions, and individually oriented or beginning family therapists are most likely to ask them. Therapists' common sense, steeped in lineal causality, leads them to ask these questions.

### Circular Questions

Second, **circular questions** also orient the therapist to the family's point of view but are based on circular causality and explore the interconnectedness of the family members:

"Cindy, which of your parents is more worried about you? Why?"
"Mr. Martin, you've been watching these battles between your wife and daughter for a long time. Would you please tell me what you've observed?"
"Mr. Martin, when these struggles start, what would you like to do, and what *do* you do?"
"Mrs. Martin and Cindy, how do you let the other person know that you're tired of fighting and want to break off contact?"
"Mrs. Martin and Cindy, if the two of you didn't fight with each other, in what other ways would you seek contact?"

Circular questions draw out the connectedness of family members and the recurrent patterns in their relationships. Rather than attempting to define the family patterns—who does what and when—the therapist uses circular questions to further explore the patterns while also raising the possibility that the family members are interconnected concerning the "problem." Circular questions, therefore, hint at circular causality and subtly expand the definition of the problem.

### Strategic Questions

**Strategic questions** are directed toward change. The therapist has determined what needs to be changed in the family and uses questions to challenge the members:

"Mr. Martin, what would happen if you backed up your wife 100% in these arguments?"
"Cindy, how will you determine whose side your father is on?"
"Mrs. Martin, how will you let your husband know that he must support you in these battles?"
"Cindy, how long are you willing to test your parents?"
"Mr. Martin, how long have you feared that Cindy is just like your brother?"

Strategic questions imply a strong and clear message from the therapist and are based on an assessment of what needs to change in the family. With these questions, the therapist moves right to the heart of the dysfunctional patterns and challenges the family members to confront them.

For these questions to have the desired effect, a therapist strongly asserts the correctness of his or her assessment and moves vigorously on the issues. When a therapist times these questions just right, the family member openly acknowledges their truth. Just as often, however, the family member may oppose the therapist's implied message. As a response, the therapist, strongly convinced on the accuracy of his or her perception, further questions and challenges the family.

**Therapist:**   Cindy, how long are you willing to test your parents?
**Cindy:**   What do you mean? I don't test them.
**Therapist:**   Well, from what I've observed, you use every opportunity to argue with your stepmother in hopes your dad will support you.
**Cindy:**   You're crazy! She's always on my back. Nothing I do is good enough, but *her* kids don't do a thing.
**Therapist:**   Then maybe I've got it wrong. You aren't testing them. Instead, you're angry at them and are protesting how unfair the rules are.

Notice that although the therapist's first hypothesis was denied, he persevered to confront Cindy on what she was thinking or feeling.

### Reflexive Questions

Finally, **reflexive questions** are formulated to trigger family members to reflect on their behavior and to consider new options. These questions assume that family members are autonomous individuals, cannot be instructed directly, and will make their own decisions about changing. Consequently, the therapist is more like a guide or coach facilitating the family members to mobilize their own problem-solving resources:

"Mr. and Mrs. Martin, what is Cindy accomplishing by her behavior?"
"Cindy, how else would you get your dad's undivided attention if you didn't fight with your stepmother?"
"Mr. Martin, what do your wife and daughter want when they fight with each other?"
"Cindy, these arguments appear to be one way you and your stepmother can make contact. Are there other ways besides fighting?"
"Mrs. Martin, is there no other way to show Cindy that you're hurt by her behavior?"

   Reflexive questions, as opposed to strategic questions, presuppose that the therapist does not have all the answers and instead is co-constructing the nature of the family's problem and the nature of the change needed *in conjunction with the family.* (See the discussion of constructionism in Chapter 3.) Tomm (1988) believes that even though these types of questions are intended to influence the family (to facilitate the family members' reflection) they are more neutral than strategic questioning because the therapist is more respectful of the family's autonomy and assumes that all perceptions have validity.
   In conclusion, Tomm (1988) argues that asking specific questions never guarantees any specific effect on the family but that circular ques-

tions, as opposed to lineal, will be more likely to engage the family and that reflexive questions, as opposed to strategic, will reduce the sense of blame in the family.

Borrowing from Tomm's classification, in assessing family patterns and attempting to engage the family, a therapist employs a combination of lineal and circular questions. (Strategic and reflexive questions will be addressed in Chapter 6, on interventions.) As we have seen, family members typically enter treatment with a lineal definition of their problem. Lineal questions, therefore, not only explore this initial definition but also facilitate engagement—the therapist is attempting to understand the family members' initial presentations. At the same time, circular questions further orient the therapist to the family patterns but also facilitate the movement to a circular, or systems, definition of the problem.

In the first several sessions with the Martins, lineal questions were first employed to understand the family members' perception of their problems: Mrs. Martin believed that Cindy was to blame for the problems, Cindy thought that her stepmother was too strict, and Mr. Martin thought that the arguments were causing the pain in the family. Circular questions were also intermixed in these sessions as the therapist began introducing the notion of circular causality to the family; that is, everyone has a part to play in the family drama.

To further specify, lineal and circular questions can be broken down into four categories:

1. questions directed toward family members' cognitions
2. questions directed toward affective responses
3. questions exploring members' motives and behaviors
4. questions asking the family members to make predictions

## Individual Members' Cognitions

Focusing on what people have been thinking accomplishes several therapeutic steps. First, the questions gather more data on the interactive patterns: Who was thinking what, and why? Second, angry family exchanges may explode quickly, with one hostile remark eliciting another. By asking people what they have been and are thinking, the therapist disrupts the emotional chain reaction. Finally, the engagement process is enhanced as family members are asked what they think, allowed to finish what they are saying (the therapist blocks interruptions), and are listened to (at least by the therapist). For example:

**Therapist:**   Mrs. Martin, you've used the word "bad" several times when referring to Cindy. I was wondering if you could tell me what you mean by that.

**Therapist:**   Cindy, certain topics appear to set you off. What are some of them, and what is particularly irritating when your stepmother brings them up?

**Therapist:**   Mr. Martin, I was wondering what you were thinking when your wife and Cindy were arguing? What actions have you thought of taking?

**Therapist:**   Robert, you look like the family observer. What do you think is going on here?

## *Affective Responses*

Exploring the affective responses reveals to what degree family members are aware of what they are feeling—that is, is there a great deal of denial?—and offers an opportunity for those feelings to be voiced. As examples:

**Therapist:**   Mr. Martin, it looked as if you were uncomfortable watching your wife and daughter argue. Would you tell me what you were feeling at that time?

**Therapist:**   Mrs. Martin, what do you feel when Cindy sleeps late in the morning?

**Therapist:**   Cindy, what hurts you in the family, and who recognizes your hurt?

**Therapist:**   Karen, at certain times you look upset in these meetings. What happens, and how does it make you feel?

Besides the cathartic effect of voicing feelings, an opportunity is presented to go past the raw surface reactions to underlying emotions:

**Therapist:**   Sometimes behind anger is a sense of hurt or disappointment. I wonder if any of you have felt that after these battles.

**Therapist:**   I know in the heat of battle it's hard to feel anything but the anger, but I was wondering if other feelings emerge after these arguments.

As a word of caution, beginning therapists frequently make the expression of feeling an end in itself. Certainly, it is a powerful effect when bottled-up emotions surface and appear as tangible evidence that the therapy is working. But the expression of emotion need not accompany a change in behavior, and, in fact, if it remains the sole focus of treatment, it may result in no change.

For example, in working with the Martins, a therapist could have a field day with all the anger floating around the room: "What do you feel now? How did that make you feel?" The session would move from anger to silence to anger to silence. At this point, one may believe that the session is productive—"People certainly are expressing what they're feeling"—but in reality the family patterns are merely reinforced and exacerbated. The Martins are fully capable of expressing anger; changing the anger is what the therapy should be about.

Moreover, continually asking for feelings—"How did that make you feel?"—can be counterproductive to feelings actually emerging, particularly in the give and take of family exchanges. Asking people what they are feeling stops them from feeling. Such a question asks people to stop, reflect, and cognitively label what they were experiencing. Not only does this hamper emotional spontaneity, but it also inhibits the family interaction.

## Exploring Motives and Behavior

Frequently, in the process of family interactions, a person is acting and reacting based on known or unknown motives and the assessment of other people's motives. For example, Mrs. Martin may believe that because her husband is so ineffectual and laissez-faire, she is the parent who must watch over and discipline Cindy. Similarly, she views Cindy's behavior as out-and-out rebellion. Cindy, on the other hand, views her stepmother's motives as purely controlling. Mr. Martin, for his part, believes that his wife is too hard on his daughter because that was how Mrs. Martin was raised.

By and large, however, people never fully articulate these motives to themselves or others. It remains, therefore, for the therapist to bring to light and explore these motives:

**Therapist:**   Cindy, your mother said that there are times when you're out of control. Have you given her any reason to think that?

**Therapist:**   Mr. Martin, your wife said she felt Cindy needed discipline. Do you agree?

**Therapist:**   Mrs. Martin, if you didn't try to guide Cindy, would your husband take over? Why?

Involving other family members in the discussion of individuals' motives aids in assessing family patterns, but it also hints at the prognosis for treatment. For example, it would be encouraging if the family members were able to listen to and comment on one another's observations without being provocative. It would be extremely positive if family members were willing to entertain another's point of view. At the other end of the spectrum, however, are families in which individual members rigidly maintain their positions, are unwilling to entertain alternatives, and continually attempt to triangle the therapist into an alliance.

Finally, exploring motives with the family members present is therapeutic in and of itself, exposing the family to new behavior. Not only does each person have the opportunity to look at his or her own motives and speculate on the motives of others, but family members have the opportunity to listen—there are no guarantees that they will—to others. Whether this promotes change or not, it is a novel experience for many families.

## Making Predictions

Another way of identifying patterns is to ask whether family members are capable of making predictions about behavior:

**Therapist:** Mrs. Martin, after you and Cindy have an argument, can you predict what will happen next?

**Therapist:** Mr. Martin, can you predict what will provoke an argument between your wife and daughter?

**Therapist:** Cindy, what could you do that would definitely set your parents off?

**Therapist:** Mrs. Martin, when will your husband try to intervene between you and your daughter? What signals does he look for?

Asking members to predict one another's behavior further details the family patterns but also explores the family's awareness of its own patterns. Moreover, suggesting that behavior can be predicted also suggests that it can be controlled and modified. Likewise, asking members to predict patterns plants a seed for change: They may have far more control over interactions than they realized.

# Case Presentation

In the first several sessions, the dysfunctional triangle involving Cindy, her father, and her stepmother stood out. The arguments were consistent and predictable:

- Cindy violates a house rule—curfew, smoking, swearing, forgetting her chores—that particularly irritates her stepmother.
- Donna Martin is offended by Cindy's behavior and believes that it is a direct affront to the family and shows a clear lack of respect.
- Confronted directly by her stepmother, Cindy is evasive and makes a series of excuses.
- Donna is hurt and offended by Cindy's obvious "lies" and begins to point them out to Cindy.
- Cindy becomes angry and yells at her stepmother, "Leave me alone." Then she leaves the house or retreats to her room.
- Depending upon the seriousness of the offense, Donna may follow Cindy to her room or try to call her back into the house.
- Cindy then swears at her stepmother and cuts off any contact.
- If Peter Martin is in the house, once the argument escalates he enters the picture, whereupon both Cindy and Donna present their cases to him.
- If he is not home, Peter will be told later of Cindy's offense by his wife and asked to do something.

- Approaching Cindy, Peter is met with her anger and her explanation.
- Unsure of what to do, Peter listens and returns to talk to Donna, who is disappointed by his lack of action.

As the presenting problem, this sequence is more than likely to be reenacted several times during the engagement phase of treatment. Beyond the seemingly automatic repetition of these patterns, they are also played out in order to establish blame and to seek alliances.

For example, Donna Martin believed Cindy was to blame for the family's problems. Cindy knew her stepmother was to blame. Peter Martin switched back and forth between the two. Robert agreed with his mother. Karen sheepishly nodded in agreement with her mother.

Closely tied to the blaming was the seeking of an alliance with the therapist: "Whose side are you on?" In the divided, conflicted Martin family, there was less a sense of wholeness and more one of taking sides. Moreover, as a new player in the game, the therapist was a neutral power waiting to be wooed, a potentially powerful ally.

In the engagement phase of treatment, the appeals for alliance may range from the emotional ("Help, I'm a victim here!") to the logical ("I've tried and tried my absolute best in the face of all this irrationality"). The emotional appeals seek out the therapist's compassion, and the logical arguments appeal to the therapist's neutrality and intellect.

Active from the beginning of the first session, these appeals seek to sway the therapist. Because their appeals are covert, family members look for signs of alliance in all aspects of the therapist's behavior: Does the therapist allow the session to be dominated by one family member's complaints? With whom does the therapist agree? (Does he or she appear to listen more to one of the members?)

In the Martins' second session, for example, a conflict erupted between Cindy and her stepmother. The argument was over restrictions Donna Martin had imposed on Cindy. After the above pattern repeated itself, Peter pointed out to his wife that perhaps her restrictions were unfair. At this point Donna began to cry, saying: "I've done all I can to make this family work. I just can't do it anymore." Her implied threat of withdrawal threatened the family and raised the tension in the session.

Silence gripped the room. Robert and Karen looked anxiously at their mother; Cindy, although still steaming, stared down at the floor; and Peter pleadingly looked to the therapist. The moment begged for someone to do something. A series of questions rushed through the therapist's head: Is Donna expressing a sincerely felt pain or crocodile tears? Is this a familiar pattern for the family? Whether this is old or new behavior, should I step in and respond to her? If I did, would this be reassuring, supportive, effective engagement or playing into the dysfunctional patterns?

As is the case in many family therapy situations, when in doubt, wait five minutes. It is highly unlikely that any behavior that occurs within the first several sessions is novel; rather, a conservative premise is to assume that the family is testing the therapeutic boundaries. Furthermore, from a systems perspective, the family is bringing into your office established patterns that have evolved to manage a variety of scenarios. Mrs. Martin's threat of emotional withdrawal is not the end of the cycle, a contradiction in terms, but rather an escalation to a more damaging level of interaction—threats of family disintegration.

By waiting, the therapist is also permitting the cycle to complete itself. For the Martins this may be a dysfunctional homeostasis, but it is all they have at this time. They sought therapy because the patterns felt endlessly frustrating and threatening. But again, the therapist is performing a balancing act. Responding to the tears runs the risk of reinforcing the patterns—"Mrs. Martin, what are you feeling right now?"—and may be seen as an alliance. But if the therapist remains passive and nonexpressive, the cycle reverberates until the end of the session, and the family members leave more frustrated than ever—a poor indicator of a second appointment. Consequently, a response is needed by the therapist. The question is what type.

One possibility for the therapist is not to be drawn into the patterns but to turn to other family members:

**Therapist:**    Mr. Martin [or any of the children], I wonder what you're feeling at this time? What choices do you have at this moment? What do you think you should do? What do you want to do?

**Therapist:**    Mrs. Martin, what do you want from your family right now?

With this response, the therapist is not only exploring the family dynamics but is also communicating the belief that the family members have the capacity to nurture one another. For the therapist to assume the nurturing role in the therapeutic system robs the family members of the opportunity to develop it themselves. Moreover, therapy may run smoothly as long as the therapist has assumed and is fulfilling a critical role in the family—that is, nurturing—but little learning or change is taking place. The family members are not developing the critical new behavior they need.

Besides the blaming and the dysfunctional father-mother-daughter triangle, other patterns are also evident and are explored via the genogram. Although briefly touched on in the first several sessions, the triangle involving Mr. Martin, Cindy, and her mother (Susan Waters) possessed a consistent pattern.

Through her biological parents' bitter separation and divorce, Cindy grew adept at playing one parent against the other. If one refused her something, she sought it from the other. When one became strict with her, she went to the other and complained—a complaint that each parent was all too ready to hear about the other. In arguments with one parent, Cindy would threaten to move in with the other.

Although this pattern could be seen as more evidence of Cindy's "bad" behavior, from a systems perspective the pattern developed and continued because of the roles the parents played. Their continued anger with each other, several years after their divorce, was highlighted by Cindy's behavior. Unable to resolve or move past their anger at each other, the parents were, unfortunately, unable to co-parent in any effective manner, and Cindy's manipulative behavior flourished.

On another level, Peter Martin's brother, Sean, was a ghost who loomed in the sessions. While constructing the genogram, Peter described his relationship with his brother as conflicted and troublesome because of Sean's alcoholism. Having seen Sean through several difficulties throughout the years, Peter had quit trying to help his brother and had cut off the relationship. Although Cindy did not remember her uncle very well, her father secretly feared that she might possess many of Sean's traits. This fear paralyzed him. On one hand, he wished to strongly guide and protect his daughter, but he feared that if he did so she would reject him and return to her mother.

Mr. Martin's ambivalence regarding Cindy was an area of conflict in his marriage. Mrs. Martin believed that Cindy needed a strong hand and urged her husband to take a stand with his daughter. Choosing not to share his secret fear, Mr. Martin excused much of Cindy's behavior, which only served to increase the marital conflict.

For her part, Mrs. Martin did not feel strong support from her husband in her conflicts with Cindy. Moreover, after a disagreement over Cindy, Mr. Martin would emotionally withdraw from his wife. Thus, Mrs. Martin was also walking a tightrope. She believed she knew what was best for Cindy but feared pushing the issue with her husband because of his subsequent withdrawal.

Compounding the marital stress was the relationship between Donna Martin and her parents. Donna had always been extremely close to her parents, sometimes visiting them four times a week. Being the oldest daughter and with her parents aging, she felt a responsibility to watch out for them.

Peter initially enjoyed Donna's family. Having lost both his own parents and being cut off from his brother, he bathed in the warmth of his in-laws. However, what was nice on a holiday became brutal every Sunday. He experienced his obligations to Donna's parents as burdensome. But being newly married and having experienced one bitter marriage breakup, he wanted with all his heart for this marriage to work. Consequently, he rarely raised any objection to visits with her family but became increasingly silent at these gatherings and withdrew to watch television.

A final issue between Mr. and Mrs. Martin was the relationships with Robert and Karen. After her first husband died, Mrs. Martin became mother and father to her children. The support from the extended family helped, but still she felt all the responsibility for her children. Thus, not only did she love Peter and want to marry him, but she also saw the possibility for her children to have a second father. Unfortunately, with all the problems,

Donna felt that her husband was completely absorbed with Cindy to the neglect of her own children. Whenever she brought up the subject with him, he said he would try, and the issue was dropped.

# *Treatment Notes*

Engaging the family members and assessing their interactive patterns are the focus of the beginning phase of therapy. We have considered the general outline for achieving these goals by adapting to the family's expressive style, using the genogram, and forming questions that guide the interview process. Each family, however, is unique and as such presents new challenges. A therapist is therefore constantly weighing what will facilitate or inhibit the engagement and assessment processes with a particular family. To simplify the discussion, however, we will examine three tasks that are performed before therapy moves into the middle phase:

1. engaging individual family members
2. understanding and respecting the family's paradigm
3. focusing on what needs to change and establishing intervention priorities

## *Engaging Individual Family Members: Therapeutic Concerns*

It is one thing to speak of engaging a family, but in concrete reality the therapist is engaging individual family members. Consequently, the therapeutic question involves whom to engage first while avoiding polarizing another family member. This is a particularly difficult task when a family enters therapy strongly divided.

The Martins are a prime example of a family polarized along family loyalty lines as well as generational ones. The therapist's task is to engage these various factions without alienating others. The central question is in what sequence to engage.

Mrs. Martin brought the family into treatment. It was only at her insistence that all the members attended. Consequently, the therapist first focuses on engaging her by listening to her and asking clarifying questions to ensure an appreciation of her position. If instead the therapist focused on Cindy's complaint in the first few sessions and attempted to negotiate more freedoms for her from her parents, Mrs. Martin would probably pull the family out of treatment: "Why go to this therapist when he's obviously being duped by Cindy?"

Because of the conflict between Mrs. Martin and Cindy, Cindy would appear to be the next person to engage. In this case, however, the therapist chooses Mr. Martin. By engaging him, the therapist first underlines the boundary between the parents and children. More importantly, to be drawn to Cindy immediately might inadvertently have reinforced the dysfunctional patterns in the family. By pursuing a more logical tack—parents to oldest child through youngest child—the therapist communicates an order to therapy and a sense that he has a plan.

As for the children, Cindy is the most problematic for the therapist. She needs to know that she will be listened to and that her opinion will be respected but also that the therapist knows that there are always two sides to a story. Additionally, the therapist communicates that he is not a judge and that who is right and who is wrong are not his concern. Rather, all family members are contributing to the problems, and all will be involved in the change process.

## Understanding and Respecting the Family's Paradigm

Mentioned earlier in Chapter 3, a family's paradigm reflects its capacity to construct its own view of reality. This view of the world guides the behavior of family members and may serve as a set of unacknowledged but powerful family rules (Reiss, 1981). With the Martins, the issues of gender, ethnicity, life cycle, and stepfamily transitions shape the behaviors of the family members.

Mrs. Martin believes that the responsibility for the family's emotional life sits squarely on her shoulders. This cultural bias burdens her unnecessarily but also reinforces her husband's frequent noninvolvement: "I let Donna handle the kids." Moreover, this unstated agreement between Mr. and Mrs. Martin intensifies the conflict with Cindy. If the turmoil in the family is Mrs. Martin's fault, it is up to her alone to solve it. It is no wonder she looks to the therapist to help her with the task of changing Cindy.

Consequently, if the therapist also shared the cultural bias, a chief focus of therapy would be changing Cindy, Mrs. Martin, or both. By recognizing the cultural bias operating within the family, the therapist does not reinforce it and avoids increasing Mrs. Martin's guilt and frustration. Instead, an alternative view is offered: Mr. Martin is also contributing to the family's emotional life, as well as Cindy, Robert, and Karen. Therapeutically, emphasizing this theme lessens the tension in the stepmother-stepdaughter conflict and opens up other options of behavior.

Raised in a traditional ethnic family, Mrs. Martin endorses many Italian family values:

1. The value system is organized primarily around protecting the family.
2. Respect for older family members is a strong norm.
3. Publically disgracing the family is a powerful taboo.
4. Independence and individuality may be interpreted as selfish and as neglecting the family (Rotunno & McGoldrick, 1982).

With these values in mind and a wish to foster a therapeutic alliance, a therapist would err by condoning or excusing Cindy's behavior. Her disrespect and behavior are an affront to Mrs. Martin. The therapist must acknowledge this fact:

**Therapist:**   Mrs. Martin, Cindy's behavior must be terribly upsetting to you. It flies in the face of everything you hold as sacred. Clearly, we must find a way for the family life to improve.

With this the therapist is acknowledging Mrs. Martin's point of view but does not conclude that Cindy must be changed. Instead, the family life is the focus.

Furthermore, as therapy progresses, the therapist remains sensitive to the issue of autonomy and family loyalty. Change will take place as Mrs. Martin begins to view Cindy's behavior as a form of adolescent maturation and realizes that she cannot expect Cindy to act as her own children do because of the differences in their backgrounds. Also, the relationship between Mrs. Martin and her parents is approached very carefully. Challenging this relationship early in treatment would jeopardize the therapeutic alliance because one of Mrs. Martin's most sacred values, loyalty to parents, would be questioned.

Even though third generation, Mr. Martin reflects many attributes of the Irish culture particularly relevant to therapy:

1. Traditional fathers are frequently uninvolved in the emotional lives of their children.
2. Husbands typically deal with wives primarily by avoidance.
3. Emotional distancing characterizes interpersonal relationships.
4. Repression of feelings is not a sign of resistance but a reflection of blocked-off inner emotions.
5. Hostility in families is generally dealt with by silent building up of resentments, culminating in cutting off relationships (McGoldrick, 1982).

Following these ethnic patterns as guidelines, some hypotheses regarding Mr. Martin's role in the family can be made:

- Mr. Martin may believe that he is a very involved father, based on cultural norms.
- Marital tension may exist because of a contrast between the spouses' definitions of intimacy. Mrs. Martin may be frustrated in her attempts to become close to her husband, and Mr. Martin may respond to his wife's overtures by distancing himself.
- The cut-off relationship between Mr. Martin and his brother hints at long-standing hostility between the two that was not openly expressed and resolved.

In building a therapeutic alliance with Mr. Martin, the therapist is walking a fine line between trying to involve him more while respecting his need for emotional distance (respecting, not condoning or accepting). Moreover, the therapist would push the family out of treatment if the marital relationship became a focus in the initial phase. The marital relationship may be addressed later, but to raise the issue in the first several sessions would increase the family's anxiety and thus raise defensiveness.

Finally, the Martins can be further understood by recognizing their stage in the life cycle and in the stepfamily transition.

Adolescence signals a transition from childhood to adulthood. Just as an individual goes through dramatic changes during these years, a family is also changing to accommodate to the emerging young adult and to prepare to launch the person into adulthood. Both Robert and Cindy have little desire to invest in building a new family; they are busy with their own developmental task of individuating from their families. Whereas Robert individuated by withdrawing from the family and becoming more involved with peers and activities, Cindy fought for her autonomy within the family.

In terms of treatment, it would be unrealistic and possibly counterproductive to attempt to increase Robert's and Cindy's bonds with the family. A therapeutic push to increase intimacy in the family would paradoxically push Robert and Cindy away from therapy. If therapy instead offers an opportunity for them to be respected as young adults with their own wants and needs, the chances of their involvement in the treatment process increase. Accordingly, Mr. and Mrs. Martin may need to be assisted in understanding this developmental process and the ways in which they can facilitate it.

Visher and Visher (1988) outline seven stages in stepfamily development: fantasy, pseudoassimilation, awareness, mobilization, action, contact, and resolution. The Martins presented a picture of a family combining the pseudoassimilation and awareness stages. Both parents saw in their new marriage an opportunity to make amends for the past and to give their children a new future, a stepfamily where everyone would get along and be happy. (It is surprising how many times stepfamilies will laughingly, but with a hint of disappointment, say, "We were going to be the Brady Bunch.") By the time the Martins contacted the therapist, they had moved past the fantasy stage and had begun to sense that things were not going well (pseudoassimilation). As each parent felt pulled by the needs of his or her own children and new spouse, there was a growing sense that changes were needed (awareness).

Contacting the therapist signaled the stepfamily's transition stage and was a positive step. Reassuring a family that what it is experiencing is well within the norms for new stepfamilies helps reduce the blaming and facilitates the engagement process.

## *What Needs to Change: Intervention Priorities*

Having built a therapeutic alliance and developed working hypotheses concerning the dysfunctional patterns in the family, the therapist by the end of the initial phase of treatment is in a position to establish intervention priorities. Before examining the specific priorities for the Martin family, several guidelines bear mentioning.

It is one thing to be ahead of the family in conceptualization but quite another to be ahead of the family in interaction. Specifically, from the first contact, a therapist is formulating working hypotheses concerning the family's functioning. Guided by theory, he or she begins to place the family's behavior within conceptual categories. In doing so, the therapist orders the clinical data, which then guide engagement and intervention strategies.

The drawback in this approach, however, is that the therapist may begin to establish agendas separate from the family's understanding or needs. With a family that presents a child-focused problem, for example, the theory may hold that the child is caught in a dysfunctional triangle with the parents and that this pattern strongly suggests marital conflict. Although ongoing therapy may prove this view correct, the family does not initially share it. Consequently, the therapist errs by focusing on the marital relationship before the couple is ready.

Many families drop out of treatment in the initial phase for this very reason—the therapist is pushing agendas the family is not ready to address. Thus, in establishing intervention priorities, one rule of thumb is: *Do not be ahead of the family; address the members' chief concerns first.*

With this rule in mind, the following intervention priorities, in order, were established for the Martins:

1. Address the dysfunctional triangular patterns among Cindy, her father, and her stepmother.
2. Clarify the relationship between Mr. Martin and his ex-wife, particularly as it affects Cindy's behavior.
3. Explore the interaction among the three parents (Mr. Martin, Mrs. Martin, and Cindy's mother) and the consequences for Cindy's behavior.
4. Focus on the marital relationship—specifically, how Cindy's behavior has affected the couple and what other issues generate conflict.
5. Identify the extended family's influence on the family—in particular, Mr. Martin's cut-off relationship with his brother and Mrs. Martin's allegiance to her parents.

First and foremost, the list of priorities addresses the issue that brought the family into treatment: Cindy's behavior. The issue, however, is the entry point into the broader family context.

In addition, it must be remembered that the list reflects the therapist's sense of priorities. In actuality, all these issues may not be addressed in the course of treatment. For example, focusing on points 1 and 2 may be sufficient to bring about the necessary change to reduce the conflict in the family. At that point in treatment the family could be quite satisfied with what has occurred and be ready to terminate. Here again, the therapist is not ahead of the family. He may strongly feel that points 3, 4, and 5 should be addressed but may recognize the change that has occurred and begin the termination process with the family.

This therapeutic balance of pushing for change but also respecting the family's limits is highlighted in the next chapter. Sensing this balance point in the course of treatment and using it for therapeutic change is a chief ingredient in the skill of conducting psychotherapy. Although the guidelines for developing this skill will be discussed in the next chapter, experience and supervision will be the ultimate teachers.

## Summary

As one begins to see, family therapy is an active process. In contrast to most individual psychotherapists, a family therapist in the initial phase of therapy is proactive rather than reactive: engaging the family members, setting therapeutic boundaries, identifying dysfunctional patterns, and establishing intervention priorities. In the engagement phase of treatment, more than any other, the therapist uses questions to set the pace of the interview. Lineal, circular, strategic, and reflexive questions not only serve diagnostic purposes but also enhance the engagement process.

For therapists trained in individual therapy, particularly the more reactive models such as client-centered, the assertiveness required of the family therapist may be disconcerting. However, with experience and supervision, your therapeutic skills are enhanced by learning to use questions to assess and intervene in family patterns.

## Glossary

**Circular question** an investigative question based on circular causality and exploring the interconnectedness of the family members.

**Genogram** a graphic representation of a multigenerational family constellation.

**Lineal question** an investigative question that assumes a lineal cause and effect.

**Norms** expectations and restrictions guiding group or family members' behavior.

**Reflexive question**   a question asking family members to reflect on their own behavior; guided by the therapist's belief that members will make their own decisions on change.

**Strategic question**   a question directed toward change by challenging the family; guided by the therapist's assumptions about what needs to change in the family.

# 5

# Middle Phase I: The Dance of Change

*Conceptualizing Change*
*Case Presentation*
*Treatment Notes*
*Summary*

Just as approaching human problems from a systems orientation broadens a therapist's assessment and intervention options, the concept of change is also expanded. Specifically, a system may change in two ways: (1) Change is continuous, and the structure (rules governing behavior) is not altered—**first order change;** (2) the system changes qualitatively and the structural rules are altered—**second order change** (Watzlawick, Weakland, & Fisch, 1974).

For example, in response to Cindy's acting-out behavior, her parents became more restrictive; punishments and limits were increased. Unfortunately, Cindy rebelled further. The family patterns became a deadly game: "You think you can control me; I will show you." It was after months of this impasse that the family sought treatment.

From a change perspective, Mr. and Mrs. Martin's responses were first order: The parents tried more of the same restrictions. Even when confronted with their own ineffectiveness, they continued with the old responses. They were responding as the rules of the system dictated—children will be controlled. What was needed, however, was a change in the system's structure (second order change). Because of their respective personal histories, Cindy would not respond to her stepmother as Robert and Karen did. Thus, what worked for Mrs. Martin in parenting Robert and Karen was not going to be effective with Cindy. Consequently, Mrs. Martin and Cindy's father needed to develop more effective means (rules) of parenting Cindy.

Family patterns are powerful in their persistence, morphostatic forces maintaining the family's status quo. When change is called for, first order change is usually tried; that is, more or less the existing patterns are employed. These commonsense reactions have worked in the past and are applied to new problems. But when first order change tactics fail to alleviate the problem, pressure builds inside the family, and the symptomatic behavior rapidly escalates. At the time of referral, Cindy was threatening to run away.

But, despite the buildup of tension and the need for relief, change is still threatening. Giving up old patterns involves unknown risks on the family's part. Yet family members are compelled to take these risks as their first order attempts at change continually fail to reduce the tension in the system. Still, therapeutic interventions may be resisted. With some families this dilemma is presented to the therapist as a double bind: "We want to make things better in our family, but we don't want to change."

This chapter discusses change and resistance by first conceptualizing change as an attempt by the family to balance morphostatic and morphogenetic forces and by describing the "dance of change" that takes place in the therapeutic alliance. The second half of the chapter employs the case example to highlight a discussion of resistance.

## Conceptualizing Change

Although all models of family therapy are concerned with the dysfunctional patterns in the family, the explanation for these patterns, goals for treatment, and conceptualization of change vary greatly (Gurman & Kniskern, 1991). For example, the models differ in terms of the perceived need for the family to have insight or understanding in order to change. At one end of the spectrum, insight is essential, as in psychodynamic models and Bowen's theory. At the other end, the strategic model, insight may occur but only after behavior has changed. Cognitive understanding may be the key to change in one model, whereas behavioral reinforcement patterns predict and control change in another.

In keeping with the tone of this book, rather than debating the merits of each theory, I address change within a broader perspective. Specifically, the family is viewed as a system moving through its life cycle while adapting to both internal and external demands. To maintain its integrity, the family must balance forces for stability—by supporting existing structures—and forces for change—by evolving new structures. Accordingly, the therapist works within the framework of the family's existing structures to facilitate the evolution of new patterns to better adapt to current needs.

### The Dance of Change: Balancing Morphostasis and Morphogenesis

From a systems perspective, as noted above, families seek to balance forces for change (morphogenesis) and forces for stability (morphostasis). Family patterns evolve to regulate these two forces. Morphostatic forces act to maintain the status quo and help provide family members with a sense of sameness and continuity—that is, family traditions. This continuity offers stability: Roles are clear within the family, and behavior follows predictable patterns. Even in a chaotic home racked by alcoholism, patterns are predictable: husband abuses alcohol and becomes abusive to wife and children; wife takes children to her mother's house; husband sobers up, apologizes, and promises it will never happen again; wife returns home, which sets the stage for a recurrence.

Nevertheless, for healthy adaptation, families must grow and change—that is, learn or develop new behavioral patterns—in response to the changing members' needs and environmental demands. For example, parenting practices for a 2-year-old differ from those for a 5-year-old, a 10-year-old, or a 15-year-old. Likewise, environmental stress—for example, the loss of a job, death, or illness—may demand new responses from the family. The family, therefore, sometimes through trial and error, learns new behaviors that facilitate adaptation and reduce stress.

Although these are complementary forces—one serves to balance the other—in families experiencing difficulties one may outweigh the other. For example, morphostatic forces may dominate to the point of stifling all growth in the family. In these families, as long as the parents are alive, a child is always a child whether the child is 5, 15, 35, or 55. The mechanisms for stability are so strong that change from accepted norms is threatening and is therefore resisted. Clinically, the family may persevere with old patterns despite the need for change. Symptoms may evolve in one or more members as pressure for change mounts within the family.

In contrast, families dominated by morphogenetic forces are constantly in flux. Nothing appears stable—that is, food may or may not be in the refrigerator, bills may or may not get paid, and, more tragically, parents may or may not parent. In the extreme this void of leadership and structure leaves the families without a solid core; they appear chaotic, disorganized, and out of control. Chronic, severe stress—alcoholism, illness, the effects of poverty—has overtaxed their capacity to cope. These families operate in a continual state of crisis management.

Well-functioning families, however, may also be pushed into morphogenetic override. For example, death, job loss, divorce, or separation may force rapid changes in a family, changes that increase stress past manageable limits. As a stepfamily, the Martins were attempting to blend two different systems with established histories into a new unit. In the process, old family structures were being applied while new patterns were also emerging. The family, at the time of referral, was in a major transition with all the accompanying stresses and strains.

To put it in more behavioral and practical terms, morphostatic forces are manifested in the family's existing interactive patterns. These patterns have evolved over time and regulate and maintain stability. Subsequently, the first response of the family to new internal or external demands is to respond with more of the same patterns. Mrs. Martin was attempting to parent Cindy as she had raised her own children.

This initial response is neither good nor bad; rather, the question is how effective it is in responding to morphogenetic requests for change. Existing family patterns may not be adequate to manage new demands (birth of a child, remarriage, divorce, last child beginning school, first child entering adolescence, parents' midlife issues, last child leaving home, elderly grandparents, illness, job loss, economic misfortune). If old patterns are able to respond effectively (first order change), then the family readily manages the new demands. But if the old patterns respond ineffectively and new patterns (second order change) are not generated, the disequilibrium (stress) becomes a chronic condition and a precursor to symptom formation in one or more family members.

Steinglass and his colleagues (1987) have identified three ways in which families fail to maintain an adequate equilibrium between the forces for stability and those for change:

1. Some families do not sense the need for change until the pressure builds past manageable limits—for example, until the depressed adolescent attempts suicide.
2. Other families may sense that something is wrong but mobilize either inappropriate or ineffective responses. In response to an acting-out, oppositional child, for example, the parents respond with harsh punishments, which only serve to increase the child's anger.
3. Some families have established an inappropriately narrow or wide range of corrective limits. That is to say, a family may accept little or no change (too narrow), which inhibits growth, or have too wide a limit, whereby members have little or no restrictions on their behavior, leaving a sense of stability greatly lacking. In alcoholic families, for example, requests for change are threatening and are met with increased rigidity. Short-term stability is maintained at the expense of long-term growth and adaptability (Steinglass, Bennett, Wolin, & Reiss, 1987).

Regardless of the ways in which the imbalance is created, the therapist's job is to assess and intervene to create a new equilibrium. Therapy, therefore, is the process of intervening and facilitating the production of new response patterns, which in turn help the family accommodate to needed change. The motivation for therapy is the family's disequilibrium and its accompanying stress. As a family therapist soon discovers, however, there is a repetition-compulsion character to old, familiar patterns. The family may rigidly cling to them in the face of powerful demands for change.

In conclusion, a therapist is faced with the dilemma of accepting a family's existing patterns (in order not to threaten the remaining sense of stability) but at the same time working with the disequilibrium to produce new patterns that will allow the family to develop more effective responses and establish a new equilibrium point. *The dance of change, therefore, is*

*the therapist's craft of facilitating the emergence of new interactive pat-*
*terns that address morphogenetic needs without overloading the family's*
*sense of stability (morphostatic needs).* Consequently, therapists are continually balancing a push for change with a respect for a family's capacity to
change. Specifically, they accomplish this balance by recognizing and working with resistances a family may present.

## Resistance

With its roots in the psychoanalytic tradition, resistance is distinguished
from a lack of motivation for change or lack of interest in forming a
relationship and, instead, is defined as an obstruction that evolves in the
process of therapy (Mishne, 1986). From a traditional psychoanalytic perspective, patients will unconsciously resist therapeutic interventions because of the implied threat of making unconscious material conscious.
Consequently, the process of "working through" resistance and uncovering
the unconscious material remains central to psychoanalytically oriented
therapies (Anderson & Stewart, 1983).

At the other end of the spectrum are experiential family therapists,
who reject the idea of resistance and speak instead of a family's differential
motivation for change, or the absence of desperation (Whitaker & Keith,
1981). In a similar vein, DeShazer (1982) argues that resistance is only a
metaphor for describing certain regularities of phenomena and that the
concept places a boundary between the therapist and family, thus splitting
the therapeutic system into imaginary oppositions and hampering treatment initiatives.

Regardless of one's theoretical position, family therapy is not a simple
matter of telling family members what they need to do to alleviate their
problem. (If it were this simple, family therapy books would be very thin
indeed!) Rather, changing ingrained family patterns is often a difficult,
two-steps-forward-and-one-back dance. For lack of a better term, resistance
has been used as a global concept to identify the roadblocks and impasses
that frequently occur in therapy. As Anderson and Stewart (1983) point out
in their classic work, "There appears to be almost universal recognition that
resistance exists, if not universal agreement about what to call it, what it is,
and what responsibility a therapist has for doing something about it" (p. 12).

As was mentioned above, experiential family therapists argue that
what has been defined as resistance is rather the family members' con-
victions that their present solution is the best available and their insistence
on continuing their patterns (Whitaker & Keith, 1981). To counter this
persistence of patterns, each family member is encouraged to change out of
his or her own initiative. Along the same lines, extended family systems
therapists, rather than working with strongly resistant family members,
may work with the most motivated member in the belief that as one

member begins to differentiate, this change will begin to ripple through the family (Bowen, 1978).

Likewise, structural family therapists do not address resistance per se but emphasize the homeostatic rules that govern how family members interrelate and thus maintain dysfunctional patterns. And in contrast, the concept of resistance is at the heart of a strategic family therapist's approach: Families come to treatment because they are at an impasse in their attempts to resolve their problems and need therapeutic intervention precisely because they are resistant to change.

In their attempt to incorporate such diverse viewpoints, Anderson and Stewart (1983) operationally define **resistance** as all those aspects of the therapeutic system (therapist, family members, organizations) that interact to prevent the therapeutic system (therapist + family) from achieving the family's goals for therapy. From their perspective, families cling to familiar behavior patterns out of habits and fears that limit their perception of the alternatives open to them. Hence, families come to therapy in response to changes that they do not like or to which they have not adjusted and are asking the therapist to restore their earlier stability.

From another perspective, Will (1983) argues that symptoms are functional and arise when a family's coping mechanisms have been unable to deal effectively with current demands. Thus, even though symptoms are not completely effective in coping with the demands, they are a better solution than the earlier anxiety state. Consequently, the therapeutic attempts to challenge the dysfunctional solutions (symptoms) are resisted because of the risk that the original problem and accompanying anxiety will reemerge.

For example, the triangle involving Donna Martin, Peter Martin, and Susan Waters was highly charged. Peter's and Susan's bitter divorce still lingered in the air years later. Donna resented Susan's continuing requests of Peter and believed that she was undercutting disciplinary efforts with Cindy. Donna wanted Peter to be more assertive with Susan by drawing firmer boundaries. Peter wanted to avoid conflict. Susan felt that Peter had gotten the better settlement in the divorce and that his recent marriage was an indication of that fact.

Although this triangle was highly charged, it was covert. On the surface, all three adults presented themselves as reasonable people who had been wronged. What would spark anger, however, was Cindy's acting-out behavior. It was as if Cindy served as a lightning rod for the tension in the system. All three adults could readily argue over who should do what to change Cindy. Of course, Cindy had her own agendas, but for the adults, her behavior was an opportunity to express anger at one another. Intuitively sensing this, Cindy would play the adults against one another by complaining to her mother about Donna, to her father about her mother, and to Donna about Susan.

Therapeutically, freeing Cindy from her role in the adult conflict would entail making the covert adult issues overt. This had been studiously avoided by Donna, Peter, and Susan. It was easier to argue about Cindy than confront their own issues. Consequently, resistance would be expected when the therapist attempted to explore the adult triangle. The adults would be happy to discuss Cindy but would be very guarded in discussing their own interpersonal relationships; the therapist's questions would be probing into a tender area. Opening up this area for discussion might be too risky for the family, and the therapist's probes would be met with defensiveness.

Will (1983) further points out that anxiety is the motivation for a family seeking therapy. The anxiety exists because the stress generated by the symptomatic behavior or its consequences becomes greater than the anxiety the symptomatic behavior is serving to avoid. In the Martin case, Cindy's acting-out behavior and conflicts between her and Mrs. Martin raised the family's anxiety and tipped the scale toward seeking therapy; the conflicts directly threatened the family's existence. Although confronting the tension in the adult triangle might also threaten the family, the step-daughter-stepmother conflicts were a more immediate and tangible threat.

As part of the therapeutic alliance, the therapist may also be a source of resistance to change. Blinded by his or her view of what the family needs to do, the therapist may confront and threaten the family's stability. A common way a therapist increases resistance to change is by trying to teach the family his or her model. The behavioral therapist may explain reinforcement patterns to the family. The Bowenian therapist may explain differentiation and the function of triangles in the family. The structural therapist may identify the inappropriate boundaries in the family. These interventions in and of themselves may be quite therapeutic *if* the family understands and accepts the therapist's observations. In these situations, both the family and therapist are "on the same wavelength," and therapy may progress rapidly.

The reverse, however, is where problems arise. The therapist shares a conceptual view of the family, but the family *resists* the viewpoint. The family may not understand what he or she is saying. Or the therapist's explanation of the problem is too threatening for the family. Or what he or she proposes raises too much anxiety in the family. Regardless of the reasons, the family resists or balks, and in doing so it is sending a message or information to the therapist.

Taking this perspective, resistance, therefore, is information sent to the therapist that the family's fragile morphostatic-morphogenetic equilibrium is being further overwhelmed. The message communicates that the new interpretations offered or new behavior the therapist is seeking are more than the family is capable of integrating *at this time*. The family may be able to "hear" the information or perform the task later, but not now!

Moreover, viewing resistance as information reduces its provocative nature (Worden, 1991). Resistance is not a threat to therapeutic progress but, rather, an intricate part of it. It is the family members' means of saying that they are being overloaded and is, therefore, a vital communication to the observant therapist. Furthermore, when seen as information, resistance does not have to be confronted or worked through but, rather, understood and responded to accordingly:

- What message is the family trying to send me?
- Am I pushing too much?
- Is the family as a whole overloaded, or just one of the members?
- Is the therapeutic relationship too weak to broach this topic at this time?
- Is the family's motivation too low to try the proposed behaviors?

## Deciphering the Message

Deciphering the family's resistance message leads the therapist to several hypotheses. First, he or she is probing into an area that is highly threatening to the family. For example, if the Martins' therapist insisted that the problem was not Cindy's but was really Peter and Donna's marital relationship, the idea would be more than the parents could assimilate, not to mention the anxiety it would raise.

A second possibility is that the therapist's direction is not understood by the family. This is a common occurrence in the early stages of therapy, when the family is confused over the therapist's request for all the members to attend: "We came here because of Cindy's behavior. Why do all of us have to attend?"

A third hypothesis is that the therapist is asking the family members to perform behaviors they do not have in their repertoire at this time. If Mr. Martin were asked to be assertive and firm with Cindy, his reluctance to do so might be resistance (fear?), but it might also indicate that he does not know how.

A final possibility is that the family members have not felt understood. While they have been busy trying to explain their problem to the therapist, the therapist has been busy explaining a theoretical model to the family. Consequently, the family members resist moving forward because they do not believe they have been understood or acknowledged in the first place.

Perhaps by now you have added a fifth or sixth hypothesis to the list. Regardless of the interpretation, however, the therapist first identifies resistance patterns and then responds to them in ways that facilitate therapeutic goals. To aid in this process, the next section returns to the Martin family and highlights resistances encountered in the middle phase of treatment. Following the case presentation, several examples of frequent resistance patterns are discussed in the section on treatment notes.

# Case Presentation

As a means of summarizing the resistance issues faced in the middle phase of treatment, this section outlines the dance of change that occurred as the Martins' therapist worked through the intervention priorities established in the initial phase of treatment (see the final section of Chapter 4). Each priority is briefly summarized, and the therapist's responses are highlighted.

### 1. Triangle Involving Cindy, Her Father, and Her Stepmother

In seeking treatment, Mr. and Mrs. Martin hoped the therapist would be able to change Cindy. Consequently, they consistently presented evidence both in and out of the sessions that she needed to be changed. For example, in the initial sessions, Cindy would pull her chair into a corner, slouch, and look bored. Occasionally she would rise out of her passive-aggressive stance and shout, "That's not true!" or "Liar!" in response to a comment someone else had made. Both of these responses had the power to draw attention to her and disrupt whatever was occurring in the session.

Outside of the sessions, Cindy continued to violate any limit her stepmother tried to set. More often than not, following a weekend, the session would begin with Mr. or Mrs. Martin complaining about what she had done or not done. The sessions began to mirror the family's home life, which was dominated by her behavior. The therapist's attempts to explore the triangle were continually short-circuited as she demanded attention.

If this pattern continued, the therapy sessions would merely repeat the family patterns, with the therapist serving as one more adult trying to control Cindy. She knew how to make the veins stand out in adults' necks and would be fully capable of countering the therapist's attempts to control her. Moreover, other issues—the marital relationship, attempts to form a stepfamily, relationships with Cindy's mother and the extended family—would never have a chance to come up. Thus, as resistance, her hostile, passive-aggressive, and acting-out behavior would deflect all other issues. For therapy to progress, her behavior demanded a therapeutic response.

In such a situation, a therapist is walking a fine line between addressing an adolescent's hostility or passive-aggressiveness and being sidetracked by it. A key, therefore, is not to pursue the obvious. For example, it was not the therapist's job to draw Cindy out or reduce her hostility but rather to change family patterns. Consequently, for him to go head-to-head with Cindy would have been akin to flying into the teeth of the family's resistance to change. To avoid being triangled into the basic patterns, several options existed for the therapist:

**Therapist** [in response to Cindy's passive-aggressive, silent withdrawal]:
Well, Cindy, something must have happened recently for you to with-

draw like this. I assume you must be angry or hurt by something but can't talk about it right now. I would love to hear what it is, but whether you tell me or not is your choice, and I can't make you talk. But unfortunately, you leave me no choice but to talk about you with your parents.

In this response, the therapist was acknowledging Cindy's behavior, speculating on the reasons for it, inviting her to participate, but also clearly communicating that the session would proceed and that she would not be the center of it.

With Cindy, this type of reaction from the therapist typically challenged her. She could not just sit back and have people talk about her. More often than not, she would pick her spot and shout, "Liar!" to counter what another family member had said. Again, this would serve to disrupt the session and refocus attention on her.

**Therapist**   [following one of Cindy's angry interruptions]: Cindy, in this office you don't yell, and in particular you don't yell, "Liar!" If you have something to say, I'd love to hear it. In fact, I think you have a lot of opinions about what's going on here, but I can't make you say them. When you want to say them let me know.

Here, the therapist was drawing a therapeutic boundary and addressing Cindy's hostility. In drawing the boundary, he was stating what was and was not permitted in the sessions. In addition, he was modeling firm behavior for the parents.

Acting-out behavior between sessions typically sets the agenda for the next session and serves to derail the focus of the therapy. In these situations the challenge for the therapist is to address the behavior but maintain the therapeutic focus. Cindy, for example, would chronically fail to follow rules established by her stepmother, which would lead to a series of arguments. By the next session, if a phone call had not already been made, the family members were eager to discuss the event:

**Therapist**   [following a heated exchange to begin the session]: Cindy, I guess you decided to test your parents again. What did you discover?

With this comment the therapist was placing Cindy's behavior in a therapeutic context: She was testing the capacity of her parents to draw a firm boundary.

**Therapist:**   I know that this weekend must have been upsetting for both of you [the parents] and that it feels as if nothing is getting better. But this was no different than what Cindy has done previously. So how did you handle it differently this time? What were your options?

The therapist was acknowledging the parents' frustration but was also avoiding being caught up in the emotionality of the event. Instead, the blow-up was used as a learning experiment for the parents. The therapeutic message to the parents was clear and consistent: You have been here before, there is nothing new, so how do you want to handle it, what are your choices? Thus, rather than being derailed, the therapist used the acting out to further therapeutic goals.

## 2. Triangle Involving Cindy and Her Parents

It was clear in the early phase of treatment that the relationship between Mr. Martin and his ex-wife (Cindy's mother) was a key to understanding Cindy's behavior. There was a sense that their divorce had been a bitter one and that Cindy, as the only child, had been triangled into her parents' lingering conflict. That is, each parent would ask Cindy questions about the other parent, and each would complain about the other to Cindy. But the hardest struggles occurred over finances. A typical scenario was Cindy requesting money for something, her mother telling her to ask her father because he had all the money, her father telling Cindy that he was giving her mother ample child support and that she was a poor money manager, leaving Cindy to go back and forth between her parents while she became angrier and angrier.

Furthermore, the three of them for years had played a game of Where Will Cindy Live? In a heated argument, Cindy's mother would yell, "Well, if you don't like it here, then move in with your father." Not to be outdone, Cindy would likewise threaten back at her mother, "I can't stand living with you; I want to live with Dad." Unfortunately, until she came to live permanently with her father, she bounced back and forth between the two households. As soon as conflicts arose at one household, she spent the night or weekend at the other.

Therapeutically, no matter how much Mr. and Mrs. Martin changed, if Cindy was continually trapped in the triangle with her parents or could play one household off against the other, few therapeutic gains would be made. Thus, the relationship between Mr. Martin and his ex-wife had to be addressed. But because of the resentment and anxiety involved, he was resistant to involving Cindy's mother.

**Therapist:**   In trying to understand Cindy's actions, it's clear to me that her mother plays a central role. Because of this I'd like to involve her in our therapy sessions. How to do this I'm not sure, and I need your guidance on this.

**Mr. Martin:**   Wait a minute! We're here because of Cindy and what's happening in our family. I don't see any reason to involve Cindy's mother.

At this point the therapist was at a choice point. Mr. Martin was sending a clear message that his ex-wife was a threatening issue and that he did not welcome her involvement. Consequently, the therapist could respect the resistance and back off of the issue. This would be a conservative position. In this case, the therapist saw Cindy's mother's involvement as crucial for change, and therefore he confronted the resistance:

**Therapist:**   I'm sorry. I didn't realize involving Cindy's mother would pose a problem. Maybe I don't fully understand the relationships between Cindy, her mother, and yourself. Would you tell me some of the history of your feelings?

Rather than backing off the issue or insisting on Mr. Martin's ex-wife's involvement and risking raising the family's anxiety, the therapist began to work through the past to the present. History is sometimes less threatening to talk about than the present, and in focusing on the past, Mr. Martin started to reveal his feelings.

To briefly summarize, Mr. Martin spoke of his continuing frustration in dealing with his ex-wife, particularly when it involved Cindy. The therapist asked him to speculate on how this conflict had affected Cindy. Building on Mr. Martin's concern, the therapist gave his own interpretation of the triangular relationships and persistently emphasized the importance of involving everyone. Having been reassured that the therapist would be in charge of conjoint sessions and that the past would not be dragged up, Mr. Martin agreed to involve Cindy's mother.

### 3. Marital Relationship

At the time of referral, both Mr. and Mrs. Martin were disillusioned and frustrated in their attempts to create a stepfamily. Financial concerns and the demands of children and extended family had begun to take their tolls on the marriage. However, the marital issues remained dormant as the problems with Cindy superseded other concerns. More to the point, the conflicts with her served as an escape valve for the family pressures.

After several sessions, the marital tension was clearly evident. Mr. and Mrs. Martin were quick to interrupt and contradict each other. If the tension became too pointed between them, however, Mrs. Martin would bring up a problem with Cindy, or Mr. Martin would withdraw. Each pattern diffused the marital tension but at the cost of not developing more effective problem-solving styles. They loved each other and desperately wanted the marriage and stepfamily to be successful. Consequently, they feared conflict between them and preferred to avoid it rather than to threaten the marriage. Over time, unfortunately, more and more hurt was piling up under the carpet.

The therapeutic question, therefore, was how to address the marital issues without raising anxiety past manageable limits and provoking strong resistance. This was accomplished by exploring the differences between them in parenting Cindy and tying these differences back into the marital relationship. After they related another crisis with Cindy, for example, the therapist asked them the following questions:

"You each seem to react to Cindy in different ways. What are some of these
    differences?"
"Are these differences reflected in parenting Robert and Karen?"
"Are these differences evident in the ways you deal with each other?"
"What has surprised each of you about the other's style of managing pro-
    blems?"
"What are some problems that have developed between the two of you
    because of the differences in your styles."

Notice the flow of these questions. They begin by focusing on the presenting problem and move to the marital relationship. The emphasis is on the
differences in style and not on who is right and who is wrong.


### 4. Extended Family's Influence

As discussed earlier, theoretical models would differ on the importance of
issues involving the extended family. For instance, Bowen adherents would
extensively employ the genogram to understand, depict, and work through
such issues that were influencing family dynamics. But because the Martins
were in a state of crisis at the time of referral and help was needed in
building the new stepfamily, pushing extended family issues would probably have provoked unnecessary resistance. They wanted immediate help
with Cindy, and extended family issues were far from their concern. Thus,
exploring these issues was low on the list of intervention priorities.

Still, the therapist was not blind to these issues and used current
events to explore the extended family's influence:

**Therapist:**   Mr. Martin, when we were constructing the genogram, you
    mentioned that Cindy reminded you of your brother. Would you tell
    me a little about him so that I can understand Cindy better?
**Therapist:**   Mrs. Martin, you said you had reared Robert and Karen just as
    you had been reared and that that was what made Cindy's behavior so
    difficult for you. Would you tell me how you were reared and how your
    parents influence you today?

Thus, rather than systematically exploring the extended family issues, the
therapist was probing these issues as they spontaneously occurred in the
session. In doing so, he was responding to the family's initiative and pursuing the issue until he met with resistance. For example, Mr. Martin readily
talked about his brother and his concern that Cindy might have many of
Sean's personality traits. But when the therapist asked him how the
relationship was between him and his brother, he became defensive:

**Mr. Martin:**   Is this [the discussion of Sean] really relevant to our problems
    with Cindy?
**Therapist:**   Perhaps and perhaps not. I'm honestly not sure. But if it's

making you uncomfortable, please tell me, because we can talk about other things.

In this exchange the therapist honestly answered the question and also communicated that this might be a relevant topic but that he respected Mr. Martin's discomfort.

Although it did not occur with the Martins, with some families after their initial complaint has been addressed and their anxiety has been reduced, extended family issues rapidly emerge to broaden the focus of therapy. Typically, the family members, with the therapist's guidance, begin to see and make their own connections between current issues and extended family issues. But again, the key is that both the therapist and family logically move in this direction.

# Treatment Notes

## Frequent Resistance Patterns

### Resistances That Challenge the Therapist's Credibility

Venturing into the family therapy waters is unsettling for a therapist in and of itself: "What am I doing? What am I looking for? Have I missed anything?" A beginning therapist is frequently more concerned with managing his or her own anxiety and getting through the session than anything else. Add in a family that is ambivalent and perhaps hostile about being there in the first place, and resistance will quickly arise. In these situations, particularly in the engagement phase, early challenges test the therapist's mettle.

Sometimes, it is as if the family senses the novice therapist's anxiety by asking such questions as:

"How long have you been doing this?"
"What does your degree mean?"
"Are you married?"
"Do you have children?"

On the surface, and in all fairness, these questions may be merely seeking information. On the other hand, if they are persistently pursued—"I'm afraid you wouldn't understand because you don't have children"—and stand as an impediment to therapeutic progression, they can be characterized as the first signs of resistance.

In these situations, the resistance message is very clear: "We're ambivalent about beginning therapy and want to test the waters." The questions, furthermore, serve the purpose of deflecting the therapist's focus from the family and permitting the family to take the measure of the therapist:

"Will the therapist be defensive? Will she be straightforward? Will she answer our questions?"

It is unreasonable to expect a new family therapist to overflow with confidence. That will come with time. In fact, as a therapist seasons, the questions just cited will rarely be asked. In the meantime, however, these challenges to the therapist's credibility may be unsettling. And more specifically, the challenges that create the most anxiety are those that the therapist has already entertained: "How can I counsel someone 20 years older than myself? How can I discuss marital problems when I'm not married or, worse yet, divorced? How can I advise parents when I don't have children of my own?"

The following list outlines a series of responses to these and similar challenges to the therapist's credibility:

**1.** *Answer directly.* Answering the family member's question simply and straightforwardly, avoiding reading more into the question than is intended, begins to establish a working relationship with the family. In this simple act, the therapist is communicating a directness and honesty in dealing with the family. Frequently, this is a more important communication than the answer. How the therapist handles the challenge speaks volumes to the family.

**2.** *Avoid defensiveness.* Immediate defensive comments (that avoid an answer)—"Why do you ask that question?"—only fuel the family's defensiveness.

**3.** *Question only after answering.* After answering the family's questions, the therapist is then in a reciprocal position to ask the family questions: "You asked me several questions about my background. I gather that information was important to you. Could you tell me why?" Again, the answer to these questions is more often than not unimportant compared with the process of the exchange. The family members are ambivalent (fearful) about entering therapy and need to test the therapist. Their resistance is information given to the therapist confirming this fact. Moreover, through testing the waters, they will hopefully be reassured that they will be dealt with fairly and that therapy will be a safe environment.

Equally important, in the reciprocal exchange of questions, the therapist begins to establish therapeutic norms: "I will be direct and honest with all of you, and I expect the same in return."

**4.** *Be aware of one's own vulnerabilities.* All therapists possess their own vulnerabilities and doubts concerning their ability to be effective. Consequently, recognizing one's vulnerabilities goes a long way toward honestly addressing them in therapy sessions. Rather than hoping the family does not challenge, for example, expect the challenge. Knowing how one will respond to these challenges eliminates the anxiety. Moreover, as the family therapist works with more and more families, it is amazing how families sense the therapist's anxiety and move right toward it. Conversely, anxiety is decreased and, surprisingly, the families do not even ask those questions when the therapist is fully and comfortably prepared to answer.

### Resistances That Co-opt the Therapist

A therapist's desire to help is also an Achilles' heel. In the effort to help, the therapist may become enmeshed with the family system and lose perspective on the overall goals. Worse yet, in this entanglement the therapist becomes part of the resistance. Two examples are the triangulation of the therapist and the family's pseudocompliance.

As mentioned in Chapter 2, triangulation occurs when the stress between two persons becomes so great that a third party is needed to siphon off the unmanageable conflict. The third party is a detour away from the conflict; for example, parents argue over their child's behavior instead of addressing their marital conflict. In other cases, the third person forms a coalition with one party against another.

In the process of therapy, both of these patterns invite the therapist into the system. For example, Mr. and Mrs. Martin can each turn to the therapist and argue their view of what needed to be done with Cindy. In this situation, the therapist is invited to choose a side or negotiate their differences. Studiously avoiding choosing a side, the therapist begins to negotiate.

Unfortunately, once on the negotiation path, a therapist is likely to be triangled into the system and unknowingly support the dysfunctional status quo. Mr. and Mrs. Martin, for example, avoid one-on-one conversations. Their communication always involves talking about or going through a third person—Cindy is the third point of the triangle. When the negotiation path is chosen, the therapist replaces Cindy and assumes her point in the triangle.

In the short run, by replacing Cindy, the therapist relieves the pressure on her and, predictably, her behavior will begin to improve. As an initial intervention this is very sound. However, if the therapist persists in mediating between Mr. and Mrs. Martin and not fostering their ability to communicate directly, the family's basic patterns are maintained: The parents do not learn how to constructively deal with each other. Worse yet, Cindy's behavioral change will persist only as long as the therapist is involved with the parents. Consequently, if therapy terminates at this point, Cindy will be reenlisted into the parental triangle.

A more insidious form of triangulation involves seducing the therapist into a coalition. For example, depending upon the therapist's predilections, more empathy may exist for one parent than for the other. Mr. Martin, for instance, could be seen as a caring husband and father who is trying to balance the demands of his daughter and his wife. Consequently, the therapist could begin to agree with Mr. Martin's position and attempt to seek Mrs. Martin's compliance with her husband's strategy for dealing with Cindy.

On the other hand, Mrs. Martin might be seen as a woman stuck in the impossible situation of trying to parent a new stepdaughter without the support of her husband. Consequently, the therapist might seek to persuade Mr. Martin to support his wife.

And finally, Cindy could be seen as the victim of the adults' conflicts. As such, the therapist could defend or excuse her behavior and subtly put the blame on the parents.

As seen in these examples, once a therapist is triangled into the conflicts, the basic system has not changed, and new patterns have not emerged. Instead, the therapist has become an additional player in the family's preexisting drama. As a result, the therapist becomes a part of the resistance to change.

The second co-opting resistance is a family's pseudocompliance. Pseudocompliance is an even more difficult resistance to notice because it occurs to the therapist only after a period of time has elapsed. Pseudocompliance is an illusion that the family members are cooperative and are engaged in the therapeutic process. The members come to the sessions regularly and on time. They politely nod in agreement with the therapist's observations or listen attentively. The therapist, in turn, looks forward to meeting with the family because of the comfort level that has been established.

In some cases, flattery from the family—"What you said last session was very helpful"—further confirms the therapist's choice of profession. The parents, in particular, are sincere and pleasant.

What begins to dawn on the therapist, however, is the family's passivity. As the therapist becomes more involved in solving the family's problems, the family becomes less active. Suggestions are met with the family members' commenting, "Well, we tried what you suggested, but it didn't work." Rather than confronting such statements as one would do with clear, noncompliant resistance (described below), the therapist is led by the family's basic cooperativeness to increase his or her activity.

In these cases, a therapist has inadvertently assumed the major responsibility for change. As a result, the family's basic patterns are not confronted or challenged. The therapist has acted on the assumption that this is a pleasant, nice, cooperative family that will follow directions. The family colludes by encouraging the therapist in these efforts. And again, he or she has now become part of the resistance to change.

With co-opting resistances, therapy does not progress and appears at an impasse. The lack of progress is a signal for the therapist to take a step back and reevaluate:

**1.** Reevaluate the definition of the problem. Sometimes the problem the family defines is unsolvable. For example, parents who want their teenage son to "have a better attitude" about his future are presenting an impossible goal, because it is couched in terms of a subjective judgment. What is a good or a bad attitude? Also, the goal of alleviating a bad attitude leaves the therapy sessions open to point-counterpoint discussions: "You have a bad attitude." "No, I don't!" "Yes, you do!" Such debates inevitably lead to the family members asking the therapist to choose a side.

2. Ask yourself what makes working with this family so comfortable or frustrating. As was mentioned above, co-opting resistances seduce the therapist into playing a role in the family drama that enhances the drama but does not rewrite it. Ironically, it is probably safe to say that when the therapy sessions are progressing smoothly, particularly from the beginning of treatment, the therapist is playing a role that supports the existing patterns. For example, if the Martins' therapist had agreed to "cure" Cindy, the parents would have comfortably sat back and waited for it to happen. Existing patterns would not have been challenged, and the parents would have waited to see what the therapist would do. Of course, without changing the existing patterns, it is highly unlikely that Cindy's behavior will improve on any lasting basis. Consequently, the initial sessions would go smoothly until a vague dissatisfaction began to settle over treatment because Cindy continued to act out.

3. Reassess goals with the family. A straightforward response to a treatment impasse is to open the issue for discussion:

"I don't know about anybody else in the room, but I have a funny feeling we're not getting anywhere. Does anyone else think that?"
"I'd like to check out with you how far we've come and where we should go from here."
"Maybe I'm missing something here. Do other people have some ideas?"
"Boy, this is really frustrating, isn't it? I'm open to some ideas."

Again, in emphasizing the importance of process, the answer to these questions is not nearly as important as the process by which they are answered: Do members participate in the discussion? Will they assume responsibility for change? Is a cooperative effort being established between the therapist and family (some indication of the success of the engagement process)? Moreover, if the family members participate in identifying the impasse and devising the solution, new patterns will be established within the therapeutic alliance (therapist + family).

### Resistances of Noncompliance

In between resistances that overtly challenge the therapist and the subtle resistances that co-opt the therapist are resistances of noncompliance. Noncompliant resistances bring progress to a halt. They communicate that the family members' anxiety is increasing and that it threatens to overwhelm them. As a strategy, noncompliance is the family's refusal to go any further.

As with the previous examples, noncompliant resistances may range from blatantly overt to quietly covert. Though many noncompliant resistances could be added to this list, four frequently occur: helplessness, pseudohostility, silence, and refusal to do assigned tasks.

Occurring in the beginning stages of treatment and likely to reappear throughout the sessions, *helplessness* is a plea from the family members to the therapist to save them (it is frequently accompanied by a crisis). As such, the family moves out of the collaborative effort with the therapist to a dependent position. The message is direct: "Help us! Not only are we powerless to change anything, but the pain is rapidly building. Do something!"

As a resistance, helplessness is very effective. The family pleads helplessness, the therapist becomes motivated by a sense of responsibility, and the tenor of therapy shifts so that the therapist is doing all the work.

At these points, a therapist may become increasingly direct with the family by offering advice or giving the members assigned tasks. For their part, the family members eagerly absorb the therapist's suggestions but return for the next session in much the same condition, whereupon the therapist offers more suggestions that, unfortunately, result in more of the same helplessness.

A variation of the same theme is the issue of *pseudohostility.* Pseudohostility is the family's capacity to quickly argue over trivial events while avoiding the underlying issues. The "hostility" can be viewed as the family's fear of intimacy; that is, the arguing is heightened when the family members move emotionally closer together. In these situations, the arguing is a smokescreen that is more easily dealt with than the basic conflicts.

Pseudohostility is evidenced when family fights are evoked with the least provocation. The simple choosing of seats in the therapist's office results in two of the children both going for the same chair, wedging themselves between the arms. At this point the children whine, "Mom, I had this seat." In turn, the parents become angry and intervene by shaking fingers at each child: "You sit in this chair now before you really catch it!"

Likewise, pseudohostility is readily apparent with recalcitrant adolescents who beg for confrontations. In these cases, anger explodes at the drop of a hat. The parents are lamenting their frustration with their sullen son when a single comment—for example, "And we don't like the friends he hangs out with"—launches the boy into a defensive tirade.

Occurring during the therapy session, pseudohostility possesses the power to rivet the therapist's attention. Whatever issue was being pursued is quickly forgotten in the heat of battle. Worse yet, the arguments invite the therapist to intervene as a mediator.

For pseudohostility to be successful as a resistance, the therapist must participate equally. The more the petty arguments absorb the therapist's attention and the more he or she attempts to negotiate a settlement, the less the underlying issues will be addressed. Unfortunately, the same patterns are played out in session after session until both the family and the therapist become frustrated with the whole experience.

Equally powerful in diverting the therapist's attention and raising anxiety are *silences.* Silences are usually much louder to the therapist's ears than pseudohostility. At least with pseudohostility, there is something to work with, whereas dealing with silences is akin to pulling teeth.

As a resistance, silence reflects the basic defensive maneuver of a young child or early adolescent. For a family to employ such a defensive posture, therefore, clearly indicates that the threatening material—for example, anger, hurt, pain, disappointment, fear—is just below the surface and that the family fears an eruption.

Here, too, for silences to be an effective resistance, the therapist must collude in the process. The family members exert tremendous pressure by simply staring at the floor or at the therapist in silence and answering questions in one word or a single sentence. For beginning therapists, in particular, any number of thoughts may run through one's head: "Oh, this is really going poorly; no one is talking." "I must do something; this is a complete failure." "What should I do; what should I do?"

Just as with the pseudohostility, in these situations the therapist is likely to become more and more energized in an attempt to have members speak. What then typically occurs is a series of dyadic conversations between the therapist and individual family members. The family interactions have ceased as the therapist works harder and harder, but to little avail.

Finally, the fourth common resistance is the family's *failure to follow the therapist's assigned task.* As will be discussed in the next chapter, therapeutic interventions are frequently assigned for the family to perform at home between the sessions; these assignments are made to further the therapeutic goals. Even with the most thorough planning and preparation, however, the family may return for the next session with a half-hearted excuse: "Well, we tried to do what you suggested, but then our daughter got sick, and my mother came over, and the kids were off from school."

Giving the family the benefit of the doubt, the therapist may assign another homework task. But if the family returns with additional excuses, he or she should assume that resistance is operating and take a step back.

The worst thing for a therapist to do is to take the family's noncompliance with assignments personally. Once the noncompliance is personalized, the therapist has engaged the family in a power struggle: "The family needs to do this assignment, and I will get them to do it." Here again, the therapist has colluded in the resistance by making the resistance the issue. In fact, one could argue that in this power struggle, the therapist has now also become resistant to change.

Consequently, the therapist changes tack and approaches the family from another direction. As a means of addressing noncompliant resistances, two steps are offered. First, stop and evaluate what is threatening the family. When resistances appear, ask yourself: "Have I been pushing a theme that the family is too uncomfortable with at this time? Has a sufficient level of trust been built up to go into this area of family conflict? Which family member is most threatened?"

Second, use judo (figuratively) to work with the resistance. As a martial art, judo uses the weight and movement of the opponent to one's advantage. So too, therapeutic judo uses resistance to enhance growth. For example, in dealing with the four types of noncompliant resistance:

**Therapist**   [in response to a plea of helplessness]: I see what you mean; these problems seem to reappear no matter what you do. You must feel terribly defeated. I must admit this is one of the most difficult situations I've had to deal with. *What do you think we should do about it?*

Notice that in this brief response the therapist is accomplishing several things. First, the family reality is acknowledged—yes, this is difficult. Second, feelings are hinted at or stated—the family must feel "defeated." Third, the therapist aligns himself with the family—this is difficult for me also. And finally, the therapeutic alliance is reinforced—what will *we* do?

**Therapist**   [in response to a family's pseudohostility]: Boy, all of you are amazing. You are some of the best fighters I've come across in a long time. How did you get so good at this?
[Or:] How will this fight end? Is someone supposed to give up, or is someone else supposed to jump in? I was just wondering, because I wanted to bring up something else.

The obvious key to these interventions is that the therapist acknowledges the argument but does not get caught up in the conflict and attempt to negotiate a settlement. Because of this, the pseudohostility is rendered ineffective in disrupting or distracting the session's focus.

**Therapist**   [in response to silences]: I think we've hit a point where it's best not to say anything to one another. I respect each of your judgments on this point, and please take my silence as a sign of respect.
[Or:] From all of your silences, I'm assuming that it's very hard for you to talk to one another. My guess is that you have a great deal to say but find the words difficult. Please know that I won't make anyone talk in these sessions and that your silence is your own choice. I believe each of you will decide when you will talk.

Again, the resistance is being acknowledged in each of these cases, but the therapist does not oppose the resistance. Instead, he gives permission for the family members to act in ways they choose and communicates that they will have the responsibility for change.

**Therapist**   [in response to the family's uncompleted task]: I guess I blew it by asking you to do that. It was probably more than you could accomplish at this time. Please, in the future, if I come up with another idea like that, let me know.

Here the therapist accepts responsibility for the uncompleted task and subtly challenges the family—it was more than you could do. Also, the therapist invites the family members to criticize future ideas he might present—resistance is thus made much more overt. As a result of this intervention, future tasks have a much greater chance for success because the family has been challenged and the task has been discussed:

**Therapist:**   You know, the last task I assigned was not a very good one; any objections to this one?

With this preparation the therapist is in a win-win position: If the family members perform the task, all well and good; if they do not perform the task, the responsibility falls clearly on their shoulders, and the agenda for the next session is set: What went wrong in trying to accomplish the task?

## *Summary*

The dance of change is the therapist's capacity to promote change while not overwhelming the family's morphostatic-morphogenetic balance. It is hypothesized that families enter therapy when the disequilibrium accompanying the need for change is more than the family can assimilate or accommodate to. Therapy is sought to break this impasse. The therapist, in turn, relying upon the tension produced by the disequilibrium as the motivation for treatment, assesses the family's existing patterns and assists the development of more effective ones.

Because change threatens the family's status quo but is required, a family enters therapy with a tenuous internal balance established between forces for change and forces to maintain the status quo. As the family and therapist begin to collaborate and form a therapeutic alliance, this tenuous balance may be threatened. Consequently, resistance to change may emerge within the treatment process in the interaction between the therapist and family.

Ironically, resistance may signify that change is occurring or that the system is recognizing the pull toward change (Anderson & Stewart, 1983). This is not to say, however, that therapy is completely resisted; rather, it is assumed that at any given point in the treatment process the anxiety level in response to threatening change may rise past manageable limits. This may be the therapist's or the family's anxiety.

In summary, the therapeutic dance of change is the rhythmic movement between the therapist and family. From the therapist's perspective, the dance requires the ability to assess patterns and discern when to push for change, when not to push, when to challenge, when to avoid issues, and so on. The treatment process thus has an air of creative tension. The underlying question in the therapist's mind is two-pronged: Is the therapeutic intervention promoting more change than the family can manage at this time, or is the intervention merely supporting the status quo and resulting in no change? Successful interventions, therefore, are based first on appreciating the existing family patterns and also on working with the disequilibrium tension to promote growth.

## *Glossary*

**First order change**   change within the parameters of existing patterns; the structure of the system does not alter.

**Resistance**   any aspect of the therapeutic system (family, therapist, situation) that interferes with the process of therapeutic change.

**Second order change**   qualitative change involving the creation of new structures and patterns in the system.

# 6

# Middle Phase II: Techniques

*Process Interventions*
*Structural Interventions*
*Historical Interventions*
*Paradoxical Prescriptions*
*Homework Assignments*
*Summary*

Conceptually, the therapist has been intervening in the family's interactive patterns from the beginning of the first interview or even the first telephone contact. And as the therapist and family form a collaborative therapeutic alliance, new patterns are evolving from the beginning moments of treatment. This chapter, however, focuses specifically on designed interventions that the therapist may employ to further the treatment goals by requiring a response from family members. These designed interventions are referred to as **techniques.**

The field of family therapy has become enamored of a plethora of techniques. Each school of thought has evolved a series of interventions to further its defined therapeutic goals. Family therapists flock to conferences and workshops hoping to find a new technique that will work wonders with those recalcitrant families back home. Techniques are wonderful tools that enhance a therapist's skill. But they are merely that, tools, which are only as good as the person using them. Moreover, they are no substitute for understanding the family: its norms, motivations, hopes, and fears.

This discussion assumes that techniques are not ends in themselves and that families do not change because of them. Instead, they are effective because the therapist matches the appropriate one with the family system at a time in treatment that captures the openings for change. Thus, although techniques can be used to facilitate the therapeutic process, their effectiveness is based on the therapist's understanding of the family and the strength of the therapeutic alliance.

The techniques in this chapter represent a basic repertoire of interventions with which most family therapists are familiar. They do not all fall under one model but instead will introduce you to a variety of possibilities. Where applicable, the theoretical model will be identified.

A number of books have collated and reviewed many of the diverse techniques used by family therapists: L'Abate, Ganahl, and Hansen (1986), Minuchin and Fishman (1981), Nelson and Trepper (1992), and Sherman and Fredman (1986). Whereas those books provide the reader with a variety of techniques, this one attempts to place the use of techniques within the ebb and flow of the therapy session.

The techniques will be illustrated by applying them to the Martin family's treatment goals. Although all of these would not be used with the same family—a bit of technique overkill—their application to the Martin family is intended to serve an instructional purpose. Finally, in integrating the process of the Martin family's therapy with a discussion of techniques, this chapter highlights the relationship between techniques and specific treatment goals. In order to refresh your memory, the intervention priorities established in Chapter 4 are:

1. Address the dysfunctional triangular patterns involving Cindy, her father, and her stepmother.
2. Clarify the relationship between Mr. Martin and his ex-wife, Susan Waters, particularly as it affects Cindy's behavior.
3. Explore the interaction among the three parents (Mr. Martin, Mrs. Martin, and Cindy's mother) and the consequences for Cindy's behavior.
4. Focus on the marital relationship—specifically, how Cindy's behavior has affected the couple and what other issues generate conflict.
5. Identify the extended family's influence on the family—in particular, Mr. Martin's cut-off relationship with his brother and Mrs. Martin's allegiance to her parents.

The techniques discussed below are grouped into five headings: process, structural, historical, paradoxical, and homework assignments. Process interventions focus on the interactive patterns occurring in the treatment sessions within which the presenting problem is embedded. Structural techniques address the interactive patterns within the context of changing the family's organizational structure. Historical interventions address the multigenerational influences on the problem behavior—that is, family-of-origin issues that underlie current dysfunctional patterns. Paradoxical techniques are used to interrupt a family's long-term, rigid, repeating patterns of behavior that are strongly resistant to change (Sherman & Fredman, 1986). Finally, homework assignments are interventions designed to continue the work of therapy in the home environment.

# *Process Interventions*

**Process interventions** are techniques that one can employ with most families in response to the here-and-now dynamics of interactions in the therapy sessions. They are particularly useful for patterns that continually repeat in the sessions and are indicative of the family patterns at home.

## *Strategic and Reflexive Questions*

In Chapter 4, a distinction was made between statements and questions. Statements set forth positions or views, whereas questions call forth positions or views. Accordingly, each school of family therapy varies in terms of the balance struck between the therapist's direct statements to the family and questions asked of the family (Tomm, 1988).

Tomm defines four types of questions used in the treatment process: lineal, circular, strategic, and reflexive. Lineal and circular questions were discussed within the assessment process (see Chapter 4). Strategic and reflexive questions, however, have direct relevance to process interventions.

The therapist asks *strategic questions* to influence the family in a specific manner. Such questions are based on the assumption that the therapist determines how the family should change. These questions, therefore, challenge and confront the family patterns:

"Peter, are you aware that you turn away from Donna when she asks for your help with Cindy?"
"Donna, you meet with continual frustration in trying to parent Cindy. Why do you continue trying in the same ways?"
"Cindy, you appear to challenge your stepmother at every opportunity. Are you aware of doing this? What do you hope to accomplish?"
"Peter, when you talk about Cindy's mother, there's an edge in your voice. I was wondering, What is that all about?"

*Reflexive questions,* in contrast, influence the family members by asking them to reflect on their patterns. The therapist endeavors to interact with the family in ways that open possibilities for the members to see new possibilities in their patterns:

"Peter, what do you think it's like for Donna as the mother in this family?"
"Donna, what dilemmas is Peter struggling with?"
"Cindy, what changes have you had to go through in the last year? How well have you managed them?"

Strategic and reflexive questions underlie a growing debate in the family therapy field. Strategic questions assume that the therapist knows what the family should change; the questions focus attention on and challenge patterns that the therapist believes should be altered. The therapist, therefore, is an expert correcting the family patterns. Reflexive questions, on the other hand, presuppose that the therapist is co-constructing the therapeutic reality with the family members, who are the "experts" on their problem, and that the therapist is simply an expert in maintaining conversations about it (Goolishian & Anderson, 1987). Accordingly, the therapist is a conversational expert asking questions from a position of "not knowing" (reflexive) rather than asking questions that demand specific answers (strategic) (Goolishian & Anderson, 1990). Within this constructivist framework, change occurs as family members have new conversations with one another rather than the same problem-oriented conversations over and over.

From my perspective, however, while promoting the resources of the family to solve their own problems, a therapist is never asking a question from a position of purely "not knowing." If this were the case, there would be little rhyme or reason to the questions. Rather, every question is guided by what the therapist deems important. Even a reflexive question directs the family's and therapist's attention and focuses the session on an aspect of family functioning.

Consequently, although the distinction is important—strategic questions directly try to change the system, whereas reflexive questions facilitate the family's own self-discovery—both lines of questioning have their place within the therapeutic process. Strategic questions pointedly direct attention to an aspect of the interactive patterns and challenge the rigid, entrenched patterns. Reflexive questions invite the family members to speculate and become aware of their own patterns.

## Increasing Family Awareness and Introducing Choice

Family awareness, akin to the concept of interpretation and insight in individual psychotherapy, refers to the family members becoming increasingly conscious of the function and circularity of their interactions (Byng-Hall & Campbell, 1981). This is not to say that the therapist presents his or her analysis to the family—"Cindy, I believe you're hurt and angry over your parents' divorce and your father's remarriage"—but rather asks reflexive questions to lead the family members into their own awareness.

Direct interpretations, as in the example above, may be satisfying to the therapist but frequently inhibit rather than facilitate treatment. First, direct interpretations imply that the therapist knows what is wrong, far more than the family does. Second, the therapist may create resistance where none existed. Cindy might reject the analysis, which she finds threatening: "I don't *have* any feelings about my parents' divorce." Third, interpretations refocus the flow of interaction from among family members to a dyadic interaction between the therapist and an individual family member. The following techniques, in contrast, highlight the family's interactive patterns and introduce the notion of choice to the family (Worden, 1991). Any one or a combination can be used.

### 1. Identifying Patterns

**Therapist:** There seems to be a consistent pattern occurring here. Cindy refuses to do something, an argument breaks out between Cindy and Donna, Donna asks Peter for help, Peter feels caught in the middle, and the argument escalates. When this occurs at home, what happens next? How does it die down?

By asking the family members *when the argument is occurring in the session* what the next step is in their fights, the therapist was exploring each person's level of awareness of his or her patterns. Not only was this diagnostic—determining who was most attuned to the patterns and at what level—but it also planted a seed of awareness that their fights had predictable patterns.

### 2. Predicting the Next Step

**Therapist** [following Cindy's irritation at Donna's complaint]: Cindy, it looked as if you just stiffened in your chair when your stepmother described what happened last weekend. You seem very sensitive to her remarks, and I have a feeling you're ready to come back at her. How do you want to reply? What do you hope to accomplish?

While predicting the next step in the sequence—Cindy's retaliation toward her stepmother—the therapist was also asking Cindy to develop alternative responses. Moreover, with these comments the therapist was stating an opinion about Cindy. At this point she could deny her sensitivity or admit it. If she denied it, she would be reluctant in future conversations to quickly retaliate toward her stepmother, in order to prove the therapist wrong. If she admitted it, the therapist could discuss her anger at her stepmother with her:

**Therapist** [following Cindy's denial]: Well, I guess I misread your reaction. If you weren't angry, what were you feeling just now?

**Therapist** [following Cindy's acknowledgment of her anger at her stepmother]: Cindy, how long have you felt this anger? Sometimes, anger is a consequence of being hurt. In what ways have you been hurt?

### 3. Encouraging the Next Step Before Its Turn

**Therapist:** Peter, Cindy just called your wife a liar. What's going to be your next response?

Rather than waiting for the next step in the sequence to occur—Peter chastising his daughter—the therapist encouraged Peter to act and to think about what he wanted to say. With this intervention, not only was the dysfunctional pattern interrupted, but Peter was also presented with a choice—How do you wish to respond—that in the previous heat of battle he did not fully realize he had.

### 4. Stopping the Sequence and Then Giving Permission to Continue

**Therapist:**  Excuse me, Donna. I think that if you keep talking about Cindy's faults, she'll soon jump in to defend herself. If that's what you want, please continue.

Again, the therapist was in a win-win position. If Donna decided that was not what she wanted, she would shift approaches, and the dysfunctional pattern would be interrupted. If she chose to continue, she would be acknowledging the pattern and making a conscious choice to carry on with the discussion and accept Cindy's reaction.

### 5. Speculating on the Motives of Others

**Therapist:**  Peter, Donna has frequently mentioned your relationship with Cindy's mother. Why do you think she raises that issue?

**Therapist:**  Donna, how does Peter try to balance the perceived demands from Cindy, Susan, and yourself? Is he successful?

Speculating on the motives of others offered several avenues to change: (1) Underlying motives were challenged, (2) perceptions were opened up for discussion, and (3) underlying issues—Peter's attempt to pacify three different people—surfaced.

All of the above interventions focus the discussion in the here and now of the therapy sessions, are reactions of the therapist to the dysfunctional process, and lead the participants into awareness of and insight into their patterns. The focus is not on the therapist's interpretations but on the family's own discovery. A basic assumption with these techniques is that awareness has greater meaning when it is *discovered* by the family (Worden, 1991).

Moreover, many of the above interventions possess a paradoxical flavor (the use of paradox is discussed below). The dysfunctional pattern is interrupted, and the family is then given permission to continue it. However, permission is contingent on the family's making a choice to continue. The message from the therapist is simple: "Here are the points where you get into trouble; if you *choose* to continue, please do so."

## *Avoiding Triangulation*

As discussed in Chapter 2, triangulation is the attempt of a conflicted dyad to involve a third person in the dispute. Within the therapeutic context, a therapist is vulnerable to the family's emotional whirlpool. The family may ask the therapist to judge who is right and who is wrong, to ally with one side against the other, to absorb the family's anxiety, and so forth. When Donna and Peter's anger had gotten to the boiling point and they had reached an impasse in dealing with each other, they would turn to the therapist for a decision about who was right and who was wrong.

More to the point, when Donna and Peter were at home and a similar disagreement erupted, they would isolate themselves in silence. Therapeutically, the impasse needed to be breached. To do so, the therapist employed each of the following:

### *1. Pushing the Sequence One Step Further*

**Therapist:**  Donna, you looked frustrated when you just turned to me. Keep talking to Peter until you clear up your frustration.

In directing the sequence of interaction one step further, the therapist was pushing the couple to break through the impasse. This intervention may or may not break the impasse but, at the very least, the therapist disrupted the dysfunctional pattern and asked the participants to display new behavior. Also, triangulation was avoided as the therapist redirected the conflict back between the dyad.

### *2. Directing the Message to the Appropriate Recipient*

**Therapist:**  Peter, you look at me when you talk about your dilemma in balancing the different demands you feel. Don't you want Donna to understand, even more than you want me to? Tell her how you see things.

**Peter:**  It's no use. She feels I give in too much to Cindy and jump when Susan calls.

**Therapist:**  Maybe that's exactly what she thinks, but try to explain it to her.

Frequently, in the course of a therapy session, family members will look to the therapist to plead their case or to tell the therapist what another family member is like. This subtle movement is an invitation for the therapist to join in the dysfunctional dance. If the therapist colludes in this, the interactions among family members become fewer and fewer, and more and more comments are directed toward the clinician. In response, as a powerful therapeutic intervention, the therapist acts like a switchboard operator, directing messages to the appropriate recipient.

This role can be accomplished in a number of ways. The therapist can use verbal comments: "Would you please speak directly to your wife?" Or the therapist can send nonverbal messages. Instead of looking toward, and thus acknowledging the speaker, he or she looks at the person to whom the message should be addressed. Or in cases where good rapport has been established, the therapist simply looks at the speaker and points a finger in the direction of the recipeint to send the message.

Simple but powerful, directing the message to the appropriate recipient is sometimes more than the family does on its own. At home, the family's interactive patterns may break down into a series of triangles and truncated conversations, or the family members may break off contact before any message is fully sent or acknowledged. By simply having the family members complete their messages, the therapist is building the family's repertoire of behavior and changing the system's interactions.

# Structural Interventions

The family's structure refers to its organizational norms: roles, power hierarchy, and boundaries among the subsystems. Or, as Minuchin (1974) writes, "Family structure is the invisible set of functional demands that organizes the ways in which family members interact" (p.51). **Structural interventions,** in turn, are designed to change these organizational patterns, in which the problem behavior is embedded.

This section is just a brief introduction into structural techniques. The wealth of these techniques is covered in the writings of structural family therapists such as Minuchin (1974), Minuchin and Fishman (1981), and Stanton and Todd (1979).

## Challenging the Family Norms

In most cases, by the time a family visits a therapist, rigid, chronic dysfunctional patterns of interaction have become embedded in the family norms, norms that maintain the family's structure. Consequently, Minuchin and Fishman (1981) observe that family therapists are alike in challenging the dysfunctional aspects of the family homeostasis but differ in terms of their methods and targets, depending upon their theoretical positions.

With the Martin family, several dysfunctional norms were clearly in evidence. First, the family's ability to effectively solve problems deteriorated rapidly into a series of mutual accusations. It was easier for the Martins to attack one another than to acknowledge the pain behind their attacks. Second, problem solving was further inhibited because the family members broke off contact with one another before resolution could be reached. Ironically, they all felt the fragility of the new stepfamily and feared the consequences of continual disagreements. It was only when things became intolerable that disagreements would be voiced. Finally, the personal feelings surrounding change and loss were not voiced. The family acted as if feelings about the past would threaten the present. (Visher & Visher, 1988, identify coping with loss and change as a first task in building a stepfamily.)

The following are various ways of challenging these family norms (Worden, 1991).

### 1. Exploring the Function of the Norms

**Therapist:** In this family, people frequently accuse one another of some misdeed or another. I was wondering, What do you gain from that?

**Therapist:** It seems important when two of you are arguing to break off contact at some point. I assume you're doing this for some reason. Would you tell me what that might be?

**Therapist:** There has been a great deal of change and loss for each of you in the last few years. Donna, you lost a husband, and Robert and Karen, a father. Peter, you've gone through a difficult divorce, and Cindy, you had to watch your parents break up. But what amazes me is I have a sense that you never talk about these things. Is there some reason for that?

**Therapist:** On top of your losses, all of you are trying to build a stepfamily, with all the changes that entails. Do you ever talk about the difficulties each of you has experienced in building this new family?

### 2. Questioning How Things Are Done

**Therapist:** I'm beginning to think that all you two [Cindy and her stepmother] do is argue. Would you tell me some of the things you've successfully talked through?

**Therapist:** Do you two [Donna and Peter] believe you're saving your marriage by not finishing a disagreement?

### 3. Challenging Each Member's Desire for Change

**Therapist:** If the three of you [Donna, Peter, and Cindy] don't start solving your disagreements, I'm afraid they'll tear the family apart. Are you really interested in change, or in deciding who's wrong?

### 4. Searching for Alternatives

**Therapist:** Cindy, can you imagine telling your father how he hurt you without first attacking your stepmother?

**Therapist:**   Peter, is there anything else you can do besides pulling away during these arguments?

A note of caution: Challenging the family's norms has the inherent risk of directly threatening the family and increasing resistance. Because of this risk, the therapist needs to have established a solid therapeutic alliance with the family. Challenges are much more accepted and entertained by the family if the members believe the therapist cares about and is honest with them.

## Reframing

As a technique, reframing is the stock and trade of many family therapists (Alexander & Parsons, 1982; DeShazer, 1982; L'Abate et al., 1986; Selvini, Palazzoli, Cecchin, Boscolo, & Prata, 1978). Moreover, positive reframing may be to family therapy what interpretation is to individual therapy (L'Abate et al., 1986).

Briefly, **reframing** is changing "the conceptual and/or emotional setting or viewpoint in relation to which a situation is experienced and [placing] it in another frame which fits the 'facts' of the same concrete situation equally well or even better, and thereby changes its entire meaning" (Watzlawick et al., 1974, p. 95). In other words, the therapist takes the family's presentation, or frame, of the "facts" and presents an alternative viewpoint. In so doing, the therapist attempts to change the meaning of what is going on without changing the facts. If he or she is successful, the problematic behavior is seen in a different light, and new patterns may then evolve.

For example, Donna's "complaints" (as Peter has framed them) can be reframed as attempts on her part to improve their marriage and family because she loves him and wants to have a better marriage and family. Likewise, his ambivalence in supporting his wife can been seen as arising out of his desire to be fair to both her and Cindy. Finally, Cindy's acting out is an attempt to discover what the rules are in the new stepfamily.

Although simple in concept, reframing is a powerful technique in freeing families from repeating dysfunctional patterns. Alexander and Parsons (1982) argue that interactions cannot shift until family members change their view of themselves and other family members. Furthermore, L'Abate and his colleagues (1986) argue that reframing is the basis of much of psychotherapy, in that changing a client's world view allows for more alternative behaviors. For instance, as long as Cindy views her stepmother as acting alone in trying to control her, she will resist Donna's "control" in her characteristic ways. Likewise, as long as Donna sees Cindy in active defiance, she must respond by trying to control Cindy.

The following are possible reframings to promote change in the Martin family:

**Therapist**  [reframing the couple's arguments]:   This marriage must be very important to each of you, because you're willing to fight for it.

**Therapist**  [reframing Peter's protection of his daughter and lack of support for his wife]: Peter, it sounds as if you're determined to make up to Cindy for the past. Your love for her is powerful. But, just like eating a gallon of ice cream, does it ever feel like too much of a good thing?

**Therapist**  [addressing the couple's mutual frustration]: I know I'm meeting the two of you at a difficult time, but there must be a lot of strength in your relationship for you to be here today.

**Therapist**  [reframing the couple's withdrawal pattern]:   I think each of you must pull away from the other during these fights because the hurt is so great and not getting through to the other person is so painful.

**Therapist**  [commenting on Cindy's acting-out behavior]:   Cindy, I think you're determined to make this family stronger by testing the limits.

**Therapist**  [in response to Peter and Donna's argument over Cindy's behavior]: Sometimes, when the two of you are arguing over Cindy's actions, I get the sense that this is the only way you can disagree and express anger.

**Therapist**  [reacting to Donna's complaint of trying to juggle the demands of the family with the needs of her parents]: Donna, it looks to me as if you're trying very hard to be a good wife, mother, and daughter. Your loyalty and sense of duty are admirable. Somehow though, I wonder if this is too much for you and if Peter feels your commitment to him.

The therapist's search for positive perspectives and motivations is at the heart of the reframing technique. If the therapist is also "stuck" on the negatives—Cindy is an acting-out teenager who is angry at her stepmother; Peter is too passive and does not support his wife; Donna is rejecting Cindy and is too controlling; Cindy's mother, Susan, constantly undermines Donna and Peter's attempts to parent Cindy—then therapy dwells on the negative, and change is therefore based on eliminating those negatives.

Instead, positive reframing focuses the therapy on developing the couple's strengths and redirecting those strengths in more productive pathways. Cindy is hurt and overwhelmed by the changes in her family and her emergence into adolescence. She needs firm limits but also a forum to voice her hurt. Peter wants to please everyone but needs to recognize that that is not always possible and that his ambivalent behavior makes the situation worse. Donna is doing the best she can in a difficult situation but needs to understand the limits of her role as stepmother. Susan has lost her only daughter and is confused about what her role should be. She needs assistance in forming this new role.

As important as it is for the therapist to see the positive and reframe behavior accordingly, the reframing will fall on deaf ears if the alternative viewpoints are presented in ways that the individual or family cannot assimilate. For example, Mrs. Martin may be so angry at Cindy for what she perceives as her disrespect that to emphasize that Cindy is testing the limits simply does not fit with her beliefs. The therapist's comments appear ludicrous and naive. However, another reframing may be readily accepted: "Donna, I think Cindy acts out when she's hurt and scared." With this reframing, the therapist may hit a responsive chord; Donna can understand being hurt and frightened.

Also, the success in using reframing lies in the timing of the intervention. Saying to Donna in the first interview that Cindy is testing the limits in the new stepfamily would probably be rejected, because Donna is just trying to tell the therapist how she views the world, and already he is subtly suggesting that she is not looking at it correctly. At this point, not only will the therapist's reframing be discounted, but worse yet, Donna will feel misunderstood. The therapist's skill, therefore, lies in the ability to look for openings and to time the intervention when it will be most likely to be heard.

Finally, reframing is successful not because the therapist is clever but because the family accepts it. A therapist convinced of his or her perceptions may be just as rigid as the family and, in an attempt to "sell" the reframing, may endanger the engagement process and raise unnecessary resistance in the family. When a reframing is effective, one typically senses immediate recognition from the family—"I never thought of it that way," or facial expressions that communicate a pleasant surprise. Thus, in the ongoing process of treatment, when a reframed perspective is not accepted by the family, the therapist quietly drops it.

## Boundary Marking

Family boundaries include the interpersonal boundaries among individual members; subsystem generational boundaries involving the sibling subsystem, parental subsystem, and extended family subsystem (grandparents, uncles, and aunts); and the entire family's boundary with the larger community. Ideally, the boundaries are permeable but at the same time protect the individual and the various subsystems.

As discussed earlier, boundaries are determined by "the rules defining who participates [in the family or subsystem], and how" (Minuchin, 1974, p. 53). They differentiate the family's subsystems. In a stepfamily, however, the boundaries are being newly formed and dramatically increase in number.

For example, what will the roles be in parenting Cindy? How much will her mother be involved? How much will her stepmother be involved? How will Mr. and Mrs. Martin evolve co-parenting responsibilities for their three children? What will the relationship be between Mr. Martin and his ex-wife? What will the relationship be between the new stepfamily and Mrs. Martin's extended family? How much time will Cindy spend at both households? And, so forth.

In a traditional family, boundaries evolve with time and as individuals' developmental needs require. A stepfamily rarely has the luxury of time. Two families come together with each member at a particular developmental stage and attempt to create boundaries agreeable to all members. A difficult task indeed!

Visher and Visher (1988) point out that a fundamental source of stress in stepfamilies is boundary ambiguity. Boundary ambiguity refers to the lack of clarity in these new structures and particularly in who is in and who is out of the family (Boss & Greenberg, 1984). Cindy, for instance, would not accept Mrs. Martin's parents as her grandparents. She rejected going to their home for a Sunday dinner. Robert and Karen felt that with their mother they were a family unit distinct from Mr. Martin and Cindy. Mr. Martin wanted one big family. Cindy, unfortunately, did not feel a part of any family unit.

Clearly, the boundary ambiguity alone would contribute to the great stress the Martins were experiencing. Consequently, a chief therapeutic intervention was **boundary marking,** to clarify and delineate as many boundaries as possible. Following are the boundaries addressed and the techniques employed.

### 1. Clarifying the Boundary Between the Households

Before Mr. Martin remarried, Cindy had a pattern of bouncing back and forth between her father's and mother's households. After one parent attempted to draw a firm limit with her, an argument would ensue, and she would pack her bags and stay with the other parent for several days. This pattern was exacerbated by the lingering bitterness between Peter and Susan.

As discussed in the previous chapter, Mr. Martin was highly resistant to involving his ex-wife in therapy and agreed only after the therapist had been fairly insistent:

**Therapist:**   Peter, there's little if any chance of changing Cindy's behavior as long as she can leave a situation before the limits have a chance to work. If some agreement isn't reached between you and Cindy's mother, you can only expect more of the same from Cindy.

Following Peter's reluctant agreement, the therapist contacted Susan, and two sessions were held with Cindy's biological parents. (The therapist decided to exclude Donna, because her presence might threaten Susan and distract from the sessions' agenda. Additionally, excluding Donna underlined the boundary of Cindy's biological parents.) The focus of the sessions was to reach an agreement whereby Cindy was not able to move back and forth.

Although the sessions were tense at times because of residual bitterness, the parents reached an agreement whereby Cindy could stay with her mother every other weekend but only on prearranged weekends.

## 2. Clarifying the Boundary Between the Former Spouses

The unresolved issues and truncated relationship between Peter and Susan were viscerally evident in the conjoint sessions. Each was quick to accuse the other of "messing up" Cindy. Each was quick to elicit the therapist's alliance. In this setting, the therapist struggled with maintaining a constructive focus on Cindy and co-parenting issues.

**Therapist:**   The anger and bitterness between the two of you are quite clear. How long has this been going on? And what have you done about it?

In response, each acknowledged that the anger was the reason for the divorce in the first place, despite marital counseling, and that things were best when they avoided each other.

**Therapist:**   That may be fine for the two of you to avoid each other, but you have a daughter to rear. And from what I can see, she's going to force the two of you to deal with each other. Now if the two of you can't put your anger on the shelf surrounding Cindy, there's little hope. Your anger will feed Cindy's anger.

Here, the therapist was challenging the parents and making a connection between their behavior and Cindy's. The responsibility for change was placed on their shoulders, not on Cindy's.

Although it would be unrealistic to expect the former spouses to resolve their differences—after previous marital counseling, divorce was their solution—they could be expected to cooperate as parents. To further their co-parenting and keep an eye on their underlying bitterness, the therapist agreed to serve as a mediator and offered conjoint sessions whenever issues with Cindy needed to be discussed.

## 3. Delineating Parenting and Children's Subsystems

In the glow of love and the hopes of beginning anew, Mr. and Mrs. Martin gave little initial thought to how they would co-parent their three stepchildren. Difficulties soon arose in several areas.

First, Peter and Donna were reared quite differently. Her emotionally involved and structured childhood contrasted sharply with his low-involvement and loosely structured upbringing. Although these differences were not a problem for them as a couple, they loomed very large when the two of them attempted to co-parent. She complained that her husband was too laid back and needed to take a more active hand with the children. He, on the other hand, felt that his wife was too strict and overcontrolling.

These differences were minimal concerning Mrs. Martin's children, Robert and Karen. She was quite comfortable parenting them as she always had, and Mr. Martin felt no need to interfere. Cindy, however, was a different matter. Mrs. Martin strongly believed that Cindy needed a tighter structure and that if Mr. Martin did not exert some authority, her own authority with her children would be undermined: "How can we have a family if Cindy gets away with things my children can't do."

To address these issues the therapist took three steps. First, he attempted to build parental boundaries by establishing a list of priorities:

**Therapist** [addressing Mr. and Mrs. Martin in a session without the children]: It's becoming clear to me that the differences in parenting styles are tearing the family apart. It would be unrealistic to think the two of you will agree on everything, but I'd like to establish some priorities in your parenting. For example, what are your expectations of each other and the children?

In establishing a priority list, rather than dealing in vague generalities, the parents were encouraged to talk out their differences and reach some agreement on what was important. The list, furthermore, served as a guide for therapy: "What are we working on now, and have we reached our goal?"

Second, the therapist encouraged the couple to make decisions jointly:

**Therapist** [again to Mr. and Mrs. Martin in a private session]: Because we can't begin to cover all the eventualities that will come up with the children, I'd like both of you to follow one basic rule for the next month: Any decision involving any of the children will be discussed and decided jointly.

By asking the parents to follow this basic rule, the therapist was, again, encouraging them to confront their differences but also to act as co-parents. Thus, the parenting boundary was being strengthened. But also, the consequences of following this basic rule were grist for the therapy sessions:

**Therapist** [the session has just started, and Mrs. Martin is relating a unilateral decision by her husband regarding Cindy]: Well it appears that our basic rule [joint decision making] wasn't a very good idea. I didn't realize it would be so hard to follow. What made it so difficult?

Notice that the therapist was taking responsibility for the poor idea and its lack of success. This was done for two reasons: (1) Peter had already been read the riot act by Donna for his slip, and he fully expected the same from the therapist. If the therapist had followed Donna's lead, the triangle would have been joined, and Peter would have assumed the role of the bad little boy who needed to make excuses: "Well, Donna wasn't home; what was I supposed to do?" This, of course, would have been more of the same dysfunctional pattern the couple had initially presented. (2) In accepting the blame for the lack of success and not provoking Peter's defenses, the therapist opened the door to a deeper understanding of his dilemma:

**Therapist**   [moving the discussion from one of blame to one of collaboration]: Peter, is this the type of situation where you feel torn between being a good father and being a good husband? If so, is there any way out of it?

The therapist's third step was to encourage the family to delineate roles and responsibilities. Who is responsible for what? Who will take care of what? How will they divide the tasks? In any organization, the clearer the roles, the smoother it runs:

**Therapist**   [with all family members present]: I'm not clear who's responsible for what around your home. I'd like to go around to each of you and have you tell me what your responsibilities are and what other people's are.

Even though disagreements would probably quickly emerge, the therapist was encouraging the family members to look at their individual roles and the roles of others. In this process, individual boundaries were highlighted.

### 4. Delineating Extended Family Boundaries

An issue just below the surface with the family was Mrs. Martin's involvement with her extended family. Although not a factor in bringing the family into treatment, it was beginning to be divisive:

**Therapist:**   It has occurred to me that in building this stepfamily, grandparents and other extended family members must play an important role. How have the extended families been integrated?

Opening the door into the issue of the extended family, the therapist was allowing the family members to first paint the picture. When the family minimized the boundary, the therapist pushed further:

**Therapist:**   I'm glad to hear it has gone so smoothly. How do you decide when to visit your parents or have them over?

Again, as with most interventions it is a matter of timing. If this is a point the family is willing to deal with, conversation readily ensues. If it is resisted, however, the therapist retreats from the issue but remains ready to bring it up at another time.

# Historical Interventions

**Historical interventions** address the past and, in particular, family-of-origin issues. Certainly of all the family therapy approaches, Bowen's family systems model best captures the richness of the influential extended family system (Bowen, 1976, 1978; Kerr & Bowen, 1988). (For a more personal account of Murray Bowen's life and theory, see Wylie, 1991.)

It would be a disservice to briefly summarize Bowen's theory and its implications for the process of family therapy. However, the genogram, directly evolved from Bowen's theory, can serve as a highly useful intervention. Detailed in Chapter 4, the genogram is a nonthreatening intervention exploring family patterns. As an objective task, the construction of the genogram allows all family members to participate. In so doing, each family member begins to express his or her point of view, and their differences can be highlighted in a nontoxic way. More importantly, the problematic behavior is then placed in the context of larger family interactions.

The genogram is a formal, structured means of historically intervening, but for the observant therapist the past can reappear at any time during the treatment process. The question, therefore, is not how to elicit the material but rather when and in what ways to use it. This section provides several guidelines for exploring historical issues.

### 1. Pursuing When the Door Is Opened

**Peter**  [in response to Donna's urging that he must be tougher with Cindy]:
    You sound just like my ex-wife.
**Donna:**  How dare you accuse me of that!

At this point, the therapist was presented with an option of whether to pursue the ongoing disagreement between Donna and Peter or to explore the historical issue just opened up. Believing that the disagreement might be reopened at any time, the therapist built on Peter's remark to explore historical themes.

**Therapist:**  Peter, I'm not sure what you meant when you said Donna sounds like your ex-wife. What were some of the issues in your first marriage?

In this example the therapist was pursuing an issue not previously mentioned in therapy. Choosing the spontaneity of the moment, he explored the issue's ramifications for the current marital interactions:

**Therapist:**  Peter, in looking back, what were some of the issues of disagreement in your first marriage, and which ones have reoccurred with Donna?

While building on spontaneity to explore historical issues, the therapist may also create his or her own openings:

**Therapist:**  Because your differences in parenting are so obvious, I wonder if you would each tell me what it was like growing up in your families? What were your parents' styles?

Or:

**Therapist:** What from your earlier marriages did you each want to repeat and avoid?

## 2. Respecting When the Door Is Closed

As quickly as a door to the past opens, a door may close. For example:

**Peter:** I don't know what my relationship with my ex-wife has to do with Donna's and my arguments.

**Therapist:** Perhaps absolutely nothing, or perhaps something. What matters is what makes sense to you, so let's stay with resolving these arguments.

Here, the therapist left open the possibility that there was a correlation between Peter's past and his current relationship with his wife but did not push the issue.

At this point, the basic therapeutic assumption was that if and when Peter's patterns in the first marriage became central to treatment, this theme would resurface. Peter's response clearly indicated that his first marriage was too threatening an issue. Consequently, the therapist underlined the point but then backed off of it.

## 3. Presenting Options for Family Members to Pursue

With historical issues, the therapist is increasing the family's awareness of patterns, tying these issues into current dynamics, and exploring options with the family members:

**Therapist:** Peter, you don't have to respond to Donna as you did to your ex-wife. You have choices! For example, what are other ways of reacting to Donna?

The therapist was building on Peter's earlier answers and challenging his patterns by asking him to brainstorm alternatives.

## 4. Respecting the Family Members' Decisions

Ultimately, the family members' decisions concerning therapeutic focus need to be respected. Historical issues may serve as a gold mine of insights and motivations for change. Or they may rapidly raise the resistance in the room and result in premature termination. A therapist lowers the risk of error by explaining the therapeutic options to the family members and then respecting their judgment:

**Therapist:** Donna and Peter, it's clear to me that a key element in your disagreements is the relationships each of you has with your family of origin and the patterns you both carry from your first marriage. If you'd like, focusing on these issues for a while may prove quite fruitful. But what do you think of doing that?

## *Paradoxical Prescriptions*

Strategic family therapists have devoted the most attention to both the theory of paradox and paradoxical techniques (Frankl, 1975; Haley, 1976; Mandanes, 1981; Papp, 1983; Selvini Palazzoli et al., 1978; Sherman & Fredman, 1986; Watzlawick et al., 1974). Referring back to the previous chapter's discussion of resistance, strategic family therapists would argue that a symptom evolves in a family in an attempt to maintain the family's threatened homeostasis. Consequently, removal of the symptom—a goal of therapy—could disrupt the family's homeostasis and is resisted. (This is particularly true with families dominated by rigid, morphostatic forces— change is threatening.) Therapists should therefore expect oppositional behavior from family members rather than cooperation. **Paradoxical techniques** assume oppositional behavior on the family's part and are based on a therapeutic paradox whereby family members are exposed to contradictory instructions from the therapist. Confronted with these contradictory instructions, family members change by either accepting or rejecting the therapist's prescriptions.

Briefly, a paradox is a contradiction that follows from logical premises and deductions. For example, to tell someone to "be spontaneous" is a paradoxical contradiction. A frequent paradox in therapy is a family's stated desire to change one member's behavior but not any other patterns, as if that member might be changed in isolation from the rest of the system. Or family members request help only to ignore the therapist's directions: "We're here because you're the expert, but we won't follow your advice."

Likewise, a therapeutic paradox (a paradoxical situation initiated by the therapist) occurs when the family expects, and is ready to reject, therapeutic direction but none is forthcoming. For example, the family members have presented their problems and wait for the therapist to offer suggestions that they will then reject. In these situations, the therapist employs therapeutic judo on the family's resistance by saying:

**Therapist:**   Because these patterns have been going on for so long, I really don't see any way of changing them. I think they'll be with you a long time. If you like, we could talk about how to try to live with them.

With this statement the therapist has hit the ball back into the family's court. The family's symptom is untenable, but threatening the status quo is more frightening to the family members. Change, therefore, is forged in this therapeutic double bind: For the family members to continue to resist the therapist—to reject the notion that they must live with their patterns—they must change their patterns.

As was discussed earlier, argumentative families have the capacity to resist and reject the therapist's attempts to negotiate a settlement. Thus, in a paradoxical approach, the therapist intervenes by saying:

**Therapist:**   I don't fully understand these arguments yet, so would you please continue them until I figure them out?

In this double bind, the family members can resist the intervention only by stopping their fights. If the fighting does continue, then the therapist thanks the family members for their cooperation; if the fighting stops, then change has occurred.

## Steps in Paradoxical Interventions

Papp (1983) describes three steps in paradoxical interventions: (1) redefining, (2) prescribing, and (3) restraining. Redefining is analogous to the reframing technique described earlier. Prescribing asks the family to do more of the same behavior. And, restraining occurs when the family shows signs of change and the therapist cautions against it.

Following are examples of paradoxical interventions employed with the Martins to disrupt their recurrent dysfunctional patterns and to facilitate the development of more productive interactions.

### 1. Redefining

**Therapist:**   I know that each of you has tried to make things better and that you feel frustrated. I've been thinking about this, and I've decided these arguments protect you. The fighting keeps all of you interacting but maintains a safe distance between you at the same time. It's as if all of you share an ambivalence about this whole stepfamily thing and move to protect one another.

**Therapist:**   Cindy, I guess you don't want your dad to get too close to Donna. You must have seen how hurt he was in the divorce and don't want him to experience that type of hurt again. Also, if you can keep them apart, maybe you won't lose your dad.

**Therapist:**   Peter, it looks to me as if you want to protect Donna from Cindy. Your hope is that if Cindy is allowed to do what she wants, she'll be happy and won't fight with Donna.

**Therapist:**   Donna, by continuing to fight with Cindy, you must want to protect Peter from these disagreements. It looks as if you take on all the tough parenting jobs to protect Peter from being hurt by Cindy.

The arguments were redefined as serving valuable functions within the family. The therapist implied that each person was colluding in this pattern and that they should continue to protect one another.

### 2. Prescribing

**Therapist:** During the next week, whenever it looks as if someone requires protection, I'd like one of you to start an argument and create a little distance between you. The argument will signal that you need distance and that someone needs protection, right now!

Building on his redefinition of the arguments, the therapist encouraged the behavior. He prescribed that the arguments would be signals that one or both parties wanted emotional distance and were seeking to protect someone. Moreover, the fights would not be spontaneous expressions of frustrations but would be planned. Consequently, he implied that if the family members could start the arguments when they chose, they would have more control over them than they initially believed.

### 3. Restraining

If the intervention is well timed and the redefining is accepted by the family, behavior changes. In the above examples the pattern could continue as long as someone believed he or she was the aggrieved party. But if a family member were seeking distance or protecting someone, the anger behind the conflict would dissipate.

**Peter** [at the next session]: I don't know what happened, but we fought a great deal less this week. In fact, we got along pretty well.
**Therapist:** Oh-oh! This makes me a little uneasy. I think this is too quick a change for people who are as good at fighting as all of you. Look, don't stop the fighting entirely. At least have several arguments between now and the next session.

With this remark, the therapist was not only staying consistent with the paradoxical approach but also reinforcing the earlier prescription. Restraining change, again, anticipated the family's resistance. Paradoxically, by resisting the therapist's admonishments to fight more, the family members were fighting less.

## Candidates for Paradoxical Techniques

Paradoxical techniques have a great deal of appeal. Powerful when successful, they would appear to offer rapid change. In the world of changing people, however, nothing is ever so straightforward. As a word of caution, resistance, and thus the expected oppositional behavior, implies that a stable homeostasis is operating within the family and that long-term, rigid, repeating patterns of behavior are dominating the interactions. Diagnostically, the family's rigid resistance patterns would recur in the initial therapy sessions. Paradoxical techniques are designed specifically for these families.

In contrast, families that require increased structure and controls (disorganized and chaotic families) are not candidates for paradox (Sherman & Fredman, 1986). These families present a lack of consistent patterns and internal structure. Examples are families experiencing divorce or the death of a parent, in which the remaining spouse is attempting to reorganize the family, or families racked by the effects of poverty and trying to meet basic survival needs. These families are not struggling with rigid patterns but are suffering because of their lack of stability.

Moreover, paradoxical techniques should not be attempted unless a strong rapport exists between the therapist and family. Without the rapport, the family members may greet the paradoxical intervention with quizzical looks and a sense that the therapist has not heard one word they have said. Or, worse yet, they may believe that the therapist is making fun of them. In these situations the therapist may feel quite clever, but the family may never return for another session.

## Variation on a Theme: Paradox and Awareness

Rather than risking a full-blown paradoxical approach and its accompanying liabilities, the therapist can combine the power of paradox with increasing the family members' awareness of their patterns through reflexive questions:

**Therapist:**  Cindy, if I told you to start a fight with your stepmother by 10 o'clock tonight, what would you do?
**Cindy:**  Well, I'd probably start by blasting my radio and keeping Karen awake.
**Therapist:**  Why would she fall for that?
**Cindy:**  She hates it when I mess with her precious Karen.
**Therapist:**  Donna, would you really fall for that?

Paradoxically, in these examples, the therapist was not focusing on stopping the arguments or negotiating their settlements, as the family expected, but instead was exploring how to start them. In the process the therapist asked Cindy to reveal her strategy and hinted that Donna would foolishly bite at the bait. By interrupting the fight sequence, the therapist forced the family members to evolve new responses to one another.

In summary, a paradoxical intervention is not a "cure" in itself, but it can help loosen rigid, entrenched behavioral patterns and open the way to change. And again, paradoxical interventions are most productive (1) with rigid, resistant patterns, (2) when the therapist has successfully assessed the dysfunctional patterns, and (3) when a trusting relationship has been established with the family.

# Homework Assignments

Family therapy does not have to be limited to the treatment sessions. In reality a great deal of "spontaneous" family therapy occurs on the family's ride to and from the therapist's office. Depending upon the stage of treatment, some families begin the session long before they arrive. Consciously or unconsciously, the anticipated anxiety of the upcoming session frequently sets the family's patterns in motion. The adolescent "forgets" to come home on time so that the family is running late. A husband and wife increase the tension between themselves on the day of their appointment.

The ride home is usually more interesting, because it is marked by silence, animated conversation continuing where the session left off, or possible angry accusations and denials: "How could you *say* that about me in front of him?" Because of this, it may be enlightening for the therapist to ask at the next session: "At the end of our last meeting several important things were said. I was wondering, What was the ride home like?"

Rather than leaving the time between sessions to the family's own devices, the therapist may attempt to continue the work of therapy in the home environment. (For example, the earlier discussion on boundary marking would be attempts to change family boundaries through assignments.) Homework assignments are very specific demands that more often than not detail precise behaviors to be performed and attempt to build skills within the family (L'Abate et al., 1986). As such, they have a strong behavioral orientation. For instance, with Donna and Peter, the therapist may ask them to return home and during the week draw up a list of household responsibilities for all of the family members: doing the dishes, doing the laundry, cleaning, food shopping. Then they are to negotiate on their own and come up with a division of labor, or to bring in the list for the next session and negotiate then.

Homework assignments are effective if they are consistent with the therapeutic goals, are clearly defined to the family, and are followed up. If therapeutic goals have been established and are agreed upon by both the therapist and family, homework assignments are a natural outgrowth and further those goals; for example, Peter and Donna wanted to learn to negotiate in better ways.

Likewise, clearly defined homework assignments are more likely to be carried out. For instance, in the above example, if the therapist had only, seemingly in passing, asked the couple to "decide who should do what around the house," the purpose of the assignment would not have been placed within the therapeutic context, too much would have been left to the discretion of the family members—if they could successfully negotiate, they would not be in therapy in the first place—and the path to the goal would have been unclear. If the therapist had not taken the time to thoroughly plan the intervention and explain it to the couple, how could they have been expected to take it seriously?

Finally, follow-up not only highlights strengths to build on and weaknesses to address in treatment but also serves as the content for the next session:

**Therapist:**   In the last session, I asked the two of you to negotiate a list of responsibilities. How did it go? What was easy? What was hard?

Or, in other words, the follow-up process served as a diagnostic tool by identifying what the family was capable and not capable of doing and underlining the areas for future interventions.

For example, if Donna and Peter successfully negotiated a list of household responsibilities, they could next be asked to negotiate the number and time of visits (boundaries) with their extended families. In contrast, if the negotiation was a complete failure and broke down into an argument, the point of breakdown would become the focus of therapy.

## Summary

The techniques outlined in this chapter are just a few of many that the field of family therapy has evolved. They were selected because of their broad appeal and ready application to a variety of clinical situations. With experience, one finds certain techniques blending well with one's personality and theoretical perspective, but a beginning family therapist is wise to develop skill with a few techniques initially and then build a repertoire.

Although techniques are frequently seductive in their appeal, particularly when one has just returned from a workshop given by an experienced therapist, they are only as good as the person using them. Minuchin and Fishman (1981) point out that although a technique is a pathway to change, it is the therapist's conceptualization of the family dynamics and the process of change that gives direction. Likewise, Sherman and Fredman (1986) argue that the value in any technique is how it is used and with what skill. Clearly, the therapist's ability to engage the family and to make an accurate assessment of the problem behavior precedes any technique.

Moreover, there is a danger in becoming too technique-oriented. Nichols (1987) warns that the indiscriminate use of techniques may serve the therapist more than the family. For example, the therapist working with the Martin family might begin to feel overwhelmed by the volatile, emotionally charged conflicts. In the face of the family's anxiety and his own, he might rapidly move to a series of techniques in an attempt to contain the mutual anxiety. Nichols points out that this rush to "techniquism" detaches the therapist from the family's pain and serves as a means for a quick fix, which rarely holds up to wear.

Still, if techniques are not viewed as ends in themselves, they have great utilitarian value to assist therapeutic movement. They may be extremely helpful in shifting perspectives within the family, increasing awareness, reorganizing the family, providing structured guidelines, and promoting change. Used judiciously, techniques are tools of the craft.

## *Glossary*

**Boundary marking**  a structural technique employed to clarify and delineate boundaries within the family.

**Historical intervention**  an intervention that explores the impact of family-of-origin dynamics on current family functioning.

**Paradoxical prescription**  a technique based on therapeutic paradox whereby family members are exposed to contradictory instructions and change by either accepting or rejecting the therapist's prescriptions.

**Process intervention**  a technique employed during a therapy session in response to here-and-now dynamics of the interactions.

**Reframing**  relabeling individual or interpersonal behavior to make it more amenable to therapeutic change.

**Structural interventions**  a technique designed to change the family's organizational patterns—that is, challenging norms, reframing, and boundary marking.

**Technique**  a planned therapeutic intervention requiring a response from the family members.

# 7

# Termination

**Treatment Summary**
**The Termination Process**
**Premature Termination**
**Dropouts**
**Summary**

The word *termination* is perhaps a misnomer in family therapy. From a family systems perspective, the therapist-family therapeutic system has reached an end point, but the family system certainly continues. From a broader view, the therapist intervenes at a moment in the family's ongoing history, helps correct the functioning patterns, and then exits. The therapist's mission, therefore, is to become obsolete as soon as possible as the family continues on its unique developmental path.

Termination also implies completion, but *completion* is a meaningless word when viewing life cycle development. The family members had problems before they entered therapy and will have problems after they leave therapy—this is called life. But hopefully, their approach to problems will be much different because of therapy.

Still, ending the therapeutic alliance is the final phase of treatment proper. This chapter addresses the decisions concerning termination: When is termination indicated? How should termination be accomplished? How can the gains made in therapy be consolidated?

As neat and tidy as termination—and, for that matter, family therapy in general—appears in books, it is rarely that in real life. More often a clinician's caseload also contains an equal amount of dropouts or cases that terminate prematurely. Managing these cases is therefore a necessary skill for a therapist and is also discussed below. Before directing attention specifically to the termination process, however, a treatment summary is in order.

# Treatment Summary

The Martins entered therapy after one year as a stepfamily. Their chief complaint was the conflict in the home surrounding Cindy, Mr. Martin's 14-year-old daughter from his first marriage. Cindy had recently come to live with her father and his new wife following several years with her mother. The escalating conflicts between Cindy and her mother, Susan Waters, precipitated her move to her father's home.

After a short time in the Martins' home, Cindy began to experience escalating conflicts with her stepmother. Perceiving her father as more "laid back" than her mother, Cindy was surprised and angered when her stepmother attempted to enforce limits on her behavior. The dysfunctional triangle involving Cindy, her father, and her stepmother dominated the assessment process.

Three evaluation sessions were held with all family members present (Mr. Martin, Cindy, Mrs. Martin, and her two children from her first marriage, Karen and Robert). Initially, both parents wanted the therapist to "fix" Cindy, giving a lineal definition to the problem. Following the evaluation sessions, however, the systemic goal established between the therapist and family was to reduce the conflict in the home and, in so doing, improve the family relationships.

In terms of the priority of intervention, the dysfunctional triangle involving Cindy, Peter, and Donna was the first to be addressed. This triangle had brought the family into treatment and was their major concern. At the same time, the functioning of this triangle underlined several dynamics operating within the family:

1. In this newly formed stepfamily, the boundaries, particularly the parental roles, were very much in flux.
2. Mr. Martin's guilt over his divorce hampered his effectiveness as a father.
3. The marital dyad was still in the forming stage (family life cycle), and the couple had not yet evolved effective problem-solving skills, particularly in the face of the challenges Cindy presented.
4. Cindy was able to exploit the split and lingering bitterness between her biological parents and to play both ends against the middle. But her acting-out behavior also reflected her pain at her parents' divorce and her father's remarriage.
5. Cultural differences between Mr. and Mrs. Martin underlayed differences in their parenting styles.
6. The cultural differences were most noticeable in Donna's anger at Cindy's "disrespectful" behavior.
7. Extended family pressures amplified the tension between Mr. and Mrs. Martin and surfaced in their interactions with Cindy—it was easier to argue about Cindy than about Donna's relationship with her parents.

In the middle phase of treatment, the sessions focused on disrupting the dysfunctional triangular patterns and facilitating the development of more functional patterns. (The specific intervention techniques were discussed in Chapter 6.) Despite this focus the dysfunctional patterns were highly resistant to change. First, Cindy's acting-out behavior frequently demanded attention. Predictably, when the treatment focus began to broaden to include marital and extended family issues, Cindy would be at the center of a family crisis.

To combat this syndrome, the therapist focused on developing and reinforcing the parental subsystem. This was done by establishing clear goals and guidelines for Mr. and Mrs. Martin as parents but also by exploring the underlying dynamics—that is, Mr. Martin's guilt, the cultural differences in marital and parenting styles, and Mrs. Martin's hurt in reaction to Cindy's testing behavior. Nevertheless, when marital issues surfaced, the parents were quick to minimize them. Clearly, the marital bond was still too fragile to absorb much scrutiny.

As Mr. and Mrs. Martin became more consistent and mutually supportive of each other in parenting, Cindy's mother was triangled into the conflict. Specifically, Cindy would complain to Susan, who would then call Peter and complain about his new wife. Peter's passivity only exacerbated the situation as all parties demanded that he do something. On top of this, Cindy would threaten to return to live with her mother.

Despite Peter's reluctance, two sessions were held between him and Susan. An agreement was reached whereby Cindy, despite her protests, would remain living with her father for six months and would visit her mother on a regular, prescribed basis. At the end of six months the living arrangement was to be reevaluated. A third session was held with Peter, Susan, and Cindy. The purpose of the meeting was to discuss the guidelines and to make sure all the parties were in agreement.

As the above dynamics were addressed and Mr. and Mrs. Martin became stronger as parents and as a couple, Cindy's acting-out behavior began to greatly diminish. There were still occasions when the old patterns would reemerge, but Mr. and Mrs. Martin were much more comfortable in managing them. Consequently, with the tension in the family lessened, it was at this point that the issue of termination was first raised.

# The Termination Process

## Who Raises the Issue, and When?

Frequently, the issue of termination is first brought up by one or more family members:

**Peter:**    I was wondering what the purpose was in continuing these sessions.

Before replying, however, the therapist questions the timing of this comment and who made it. For instance, the question may be raised at a particularly difficult time in therapy and may strongly reflect the family's resistance. Or the question may be raised by a family member who has been consistently defensive and resistant.

If the Martins' therapist concluded that the question of termination was premature, he would see Peter's statement as resistance and as an expression of Peter's discomfort with the focus of treatment:

**Therapist:**    Peter, I think the question of termination is a legitimate issue and needs to be discussed, particularly in light of how far all of you have come as a family. However, I may be wrong, but I think we're right in the middle of something and not at the end of it.

Peter Martin's introducing the issue of termination was both indicative of resistance and a recognition that therapy had accomplished the initial goals. Cindy's behavior had significantly improved but from the therapist's perspective, the underlying marital and extended family issues potentially threatened the stepfamily's evolution. In addition, the unaddressed marital conflict had the potential to triangle Cindy into future covert disagreements. Nevertheless, when the therapist began to probe the covert marital issues, both Peter and Donna quickly united to seal over any differences. They believed they could now function better as parents and were pleased with the progress they had made with Cindy. The marital differences the therapist was pointing out were not a problem.

In this situation, having accomplished the initial, specific goals of therapy and in the face of Peter and Donna's satisfaction with what had occurred and reluctance to go further, the therapist began consolidating the gains made in therapy (a process detailed below) and terminated with the family.

## Have Specific Goals Been Met?

On the most basic level the question of termination is very simple: Has the chief complaint been resolved, and have the initial goals established for treatment been met? If this is the case, the treatment process has come full cycle, and the initial goals have led to a clear termination point.

Clearly established goals serve as a beacon throughout treatment, but they are invaluable at termination. The question of whether to end the sessions becomes straightforward: Are the family members satisfied with the progress they have made toward their goals?

Another guide is the therapist's theoretical model. For strategic and behavioral-oriented family therapists, problem resolution is the end in itself and signals termination. Structural therapists emphasize the reorganization of the family's structure and the family's ability to nurture and support its members. Psychoanalytic family therapists are concerned with the emergence and resolution of unconscious processes. Bowenian therapists assess the increase in differentiation within the family and the changes in family-of-origin relationships.

As always, the therapist's agenda may conflict with the family's. The family may reach a point where further sessions are not warranted, whereas the therapist, staying within a conceptual model, may see much more work to be done. Certainly the therapist needs to raise concerns and point out the areas where more work is needed, but in the final analysis the family makes the decision.

In taking this position, the therapist not only communicates respect for the family but also leaves the door open for future contacts. The fastest way to burn any future bridges is for the therapist to resist the family's request for termination and to doggedly point out all the additional work needed. This not only diminishes the family's work to this point but also pushes the family into an oppositional stance: The family members must demonstrate that they are ready to terminate by sealing over problems. Worse yet, the family may be very reluctant to return to the therapist in the future because of the therapist's implied "I told you so."

With the Martins, the therapist clearly saw a need for additional therapeutic work pertaining to the marital dynamics and extended family issues. Nevertheless, the initial goals had been accomplished, and the family did not wish to go any further. Of course, the therapist could have pushed for further sessions and "confronted" the family members with their resistance, but this would have only served to drive a wedge in the therapeutic alliance. And from another perspective, perhaps Peter and Donna were wise not to go into their marital dynamics at this time. Perhaps they needed first to experience more success as a parental team, which in turn would reduce the pressure on their marriage. As always, the element of timing must be respected.

Thus, rather than staying within one's theoretical position to determine the timing of termination, one can take a broader view and ask the following questions:

(1) Is there a reduction in the symptom behavior?
(2) Have the family members made basic changes in their interactions concerning the symptom area?
(3) Do they possess some knowledge of the circularity of their interactions?
(4) Is the family on its way to new rules of problem solving?

## How Can Gains Be Consolidated?

Deciding that termination is the next logical step in the treatment process, the therapist proceeds through a termination sequence designed to consolidate the gains made in therapy and to leave the door open for future contacts.

### 1. Taking Inventory

The first step in this sequence is akin to taking inventory. Each family member is asked what has changed, and then all are asked to comment on what the others have said:

**Therapist:**   As a way of ending our sessions, I'd like to go around the room and ask each of you what changes you see in the family.

At this point, the Martins' therapist engaged each family member, drawing them out and asking clarifying questions. His purpose was to explore the various points of view and to highlight similarities and differences among the participants:

**Therapist:**   Peter, you agree with Donna that the two of you are now more effective as parents. Would you give me some examples of this?

**Therapist** [addressing Peter and Donna]: What has helped you become more effective as parents?

After each family member had spoken, the therapist asked them to comment on what others had said. On a diagnostic level the therapist observed how difficult or easy this was to do: Did the family members readily and easily interact with one another? How were differences managed? On a process level the family members were consolidating their gains by exploring one another's perspectives.

### 2. Providing Understanding

The therapist is now in a position to share with the family his or her own impressions of the changes that have taken place. Here, the therapist may offer a conceptual understanding of the changes in the family:

**Therapist:**   I believe as parents you have drawn a clearer boundary between yourselves and the children and the in-laws.

Or a more concrete explanation:

**Therapist:**   You two have really begun to act like effective parents, and I think it shows throughout the family.

**Therapist:**   Peter, I know it has been difficult drawing a firmer line with Cindy, but I think you've succeeded wonderfully. What has helped you do this? How has Donna helped with this, and what can she do in the future?

**Therapist:**   As the two of you have become more consistent with Cindy, I believe she has come to trust that she can rely on both of you to be firm and fair. In the process you have made her world a more secure place.

**Therapist:**   Cindy, I give you a world of credit. It hasn't been easy for you, given all you've been through over the past several years. I must say how impressed I've been at your ability to express your hurt and anger but in more productive ways.

In this exchange of impressions the therapist was in a position to consolidate change by highlighting the key elements and providing the family with an understanding of those changes. This cognitive labeling enabled the family to take something concrete from therapy that could serve as a reminder and guideline in future situations. Or, as Bandler, Grinder, and Satir (1976) point out, the outcome of family therapy is not simply an experience that the members can use but also an understanding of that experience and specific tools to enhance their own growth.

### 3. Speculating on the Future

The next step combines termination and a therapeutic intervention whereby the therapist and family outline future pitfalls facing the family:

**Therapist:**  I think we have a sense of where we've been, but I was wondering if we could look into the future. What might happen that would test the changes you've made? What do you think will be next in your development as a stepfamily?

**Therapist:**  Can the two of you [Donna and Peter] imagine any issue that could arise in parenting your children where you might disagree?

**Therapist:**  What would stop the two of you from reaching an agreement? If you were in a marital argument, would this interfere with you being parents?

**Therapist:**  Cindy, can you imagine anything in the future you and your stepmother might argue about?

As a prophylactic measure the therapist was exploring the possible pitfalls that awaited the family. Playing the devil's advocate, he challenged the family's ability to manage future conflicts:

**Therapist:**  I hope none of these events [the future pitfalls] occur, but I'm a strong believer in preparing for the worst.

Paradoxically, by challenging the changes made so far in the family and predicting future pitfalls, the therapist was cementing the change to this point and stiffening the family's resolve to maintain those changes. Thus, he was not only building in a prophylactic trip wire but also intervening in a paradoxical fashion.

### 4. Eliciting Feedback

Termination offers the therapist an opportunity to learn. By asking the family members what was helpful and not helpful during treatment, the therapist builds a personal data base. It is quite surprising sometimes to hear what each family member has found helpful. What the therapist was intending and what the family found useful may be quite different. There are, furthermore, as many different responses as there are family members. But regardless, each will have something unique to add.

Also, by asking the family members for feedback, the therapist gains an appreciation of his or her personal style. Though they may have the same theoretical position, no two therapists conduct therapy in quite the same way. Knowingly or unknowingly, every therapist develops a unique style. Fortunately for the therapist open to it, the family's feedback offers the opportunity to learn what is effective and not effective in one's style.

### 5. Leaving the Door Open for Future Contacts

As mentioned above, from a systems, life cycle perspective, families are in constant evolution. Thus, problems will continually present themselves. Ideally, what has been learned in therapy will be applied to future situations, but the unexpected will always occur. Consequently, the therapist leaves the door open for future contacts.

**Therapist:**   Before we close, I just wanted to say that I'd be happy to meet with any or all of you in the future. Please feel free to contact me.

It is not uncommon for a therapist to be recontacted by a family a number of years later. Sometimes it is because old patterns have reemerged. Sometimes the next developmental stage presents challenges that appear overwhelming to the family. Sometimes it is a simple one-session checkup. Whatever the reason, termination sets the stage and extends the invitation for future contact.

## *Premature Termination*

As described above, in many situations the family raises the issue of termination in the middle of the treatment process (as the therapist perceives it). Frequently, the issue is raised as a complaint. The therapist's first response is to address it as resistance and weigh the family's reaction:

**Peter**   [after four sessions when Cindy has begun an intense testing of the parents' new limits]: Things have become worse, not better, since we've been coming here! I don't know if we should keep coming or not.

**Therapist:**   Whether you come or not has always been your decision. But your frustration may be a result of trying to learn something new. Cindy's certainly going to test these new limits, and I think she's wondering which way you'll go.

At other times, however, the threat of premature termination raises the *therapist's* anxiety. Instead of addressing the complaint as resistance, the therapist may fear losing the case and therefore collude in the resistance. For instance, in the above example, the therapist could have backed off the therapeutic focus on the couple and returned to focusing solely on Cindy. In the short run this would have reduced Peter's anxiety, and he would have continued the sessions. However, he probably would have continued only as long as the therapist focused on his daughter and asked little of him. Thus, the eventual shift to the broader system would probably have again raised Peter's anxiety.

At these points in treatment, the therapist's art and intuition enter the picture in determining if the therapeutic focus is too threatening to the family: "Should I continue to push the parental and marital issues or shift back to the initial focus on Cindy? Will the family be able to absorb an increase in anxiety, or am I pushing them to drop out? Is there a way of reframing the shift to the parental issues that will be more acceptable to Peter?"

As was outlined above, the most straightforward means of addressing premature termination is to respect the family's opinion but also identify the future pitfalls and further obstacles to change and to leave an open door for the family. Rather than judging these families as resistant and confronting their resistance, the therapist views them from a developmental perspective and considers the element of timing. Although Peter and Donna were reluctant to discuss their covert marital conflict at the time, they would be more likely to resume therapy at a later date if the therapist planted the seed (the marital relationship) and terminated, even though prematurely, on good terms.

## *Dropouts*

Several missed appointments, explained by questionable excuses, begin to hint that a family is ready to drop out of treatment. At the close of a session, a family member explains to the therapist, "I don't know our plans for next week, so I'll give you a call to schedule the next appointment." The phone call never comes. Or the family simply fails to come to a scheduled appointment and does not bother to call. Each of these signals a dropout.

Dropouts may occur in any phase of treatment. Sometimes they occur in the early phase of treatment because of a lack of engagement between the family and therapist. This may be due to an initial low level of motivation on the family's part, the therapist's inability to engage the family, or both. Sometimes dropping out occurs in the middle phases of treatment as the family's anxiety is pushed past manageable limits and withdrawal is the last defense.

Dropouts are a fact of life for even the most experienced family therapist. Masters (1978) reports on a study in which only highly motivated families were selected for treatment. Despite the rigid screening procedures, 40% of the families dropped out after six to ten sessions. Thus, even maximizing the possibilities for success by controlling for motivation, dropouts still occurred—a humbling thought!

Of course, the rest of us do not have the luxury of a controlled study to screen out our clients. Families come into our offices with a wide variety of problems and motivations. To believe we will engage each and every family and successfully terminate therapy borders on hubris. Still, dropouts can be minimized.

First, a thorough assessment phase in and of itself not only tests the family's motivation for therapy but also enhances the engagement process. In the assessment phase, how open the family is to the therapist's questions is an initial indication of motivation: Does the family readily respond to the questions? Are the members honest and straightforward in their responses? Are they guarded and suspicious? Are they apathetic or indifferent?

Sometimes a family's poor motivation can be overcome by a successful engagement between the family and therapist. In these cases, a therapeutic alliance is formed as the family members believe the therapist understands them and appreciates their struggles. When engagement is difficult and the family appears reluctant or ambivalent concerning therapy, however, it is best for the therapist to put the issue on the table:

**Therapist:**    Through our conversations I have a good sense of the problems you face as a family, but I also have a sense that some of you are not sure about this therapy business. I believe it would be helpful if we could discuss some of these concerns.

The therapist is not only addressing the ambivalence but also developing a therapeutic alliance. Paradoxically, as the family members honestly discuss their ambivalence and reluctance to begin therapy, they are developing a therapeutic bond with the therapist: "We agree to disagree and will be honest in the process" (Worden, 1991).

Of course, this tactic works only as long as the therapist is open to hearing the family's reluctance and not afraid of the family dropping out. With this stance, the therapist communicates a respect for the family members' concerns and a willingness to accept their decision about beginning therapy, whatever it might be. In particular, this is a vital message to families struggling with control issues. Not only are they experiencing internal control battles, but the last thing they need is a control battle with the therapist over whether to begin therapy.

In situations where the family has canceled or not shown up for several appointments, a follow-up call is in order. Although with a follow-up call the therapist is walking a fine line between chasing a reluctant family and encouraging the engagement process, he or she is communicating concern and willingness to work with the family. Consequently, rather than asking the family member why he or she has canceled the appointments or has not called, and possibly putting that person on the defensive, the therapist wants to make sure he or she is understood:

**Therapist**    [in a follow-up call]: I'm calling because you've canceled several of our appointments. I was wondering if some difficulties have come up, and I was also wondering if I was unclear about the purpose of our meetings.

The therapist is expressing concern for the family and asking whether he or she has been clear. Moreover, the therapist has expressed a desire to meet the family halfway and to open a dialogue with the family member.

Dropouts, however, may raise a therapist's anxiety. In some cases pathology is so prevalent—severe acting out, suicide potential, substance abuse—and the family's defensive denial is so powerful that engaging the family is quite difficult. This is particularly true with families that are not self-referred but are coerced into therapy (for example, by school or legal authorities). These families may go through the motions of attending several sessions (usually until they believe they have satisfied the external authority) and then drop out. The therapist, however, is left feeling helpless and in a quandary. "Do I bother calling the family? Do I notify the referral source? Do I try to convince the family of the severity of their problems?"

As an aside, with families coerced into treatment by an external authority, it is important and saves needless worry to address the issue of coercion in the first session. Clarifying the role of the therapist in relationship to the referring authority—for example, having the family sign the necessary release-of-information forms—is part of the contract with the family. Thus, if the family does drop out, the therapist is clear on whether to involve the referral source as per the earlier agreement:

**Therapist** [to the family members]: What is the agreement you have with the school [or probation officer] about being in therapy? For example, how many sessions are you supposed to attend? What is the problem you were referred for?

**Therapist:** Also, before we begin any meetings, I'd like to call the person who referred you and be clear on my responsibilities in working with you.

If, however, the therapist has been unable to telephone the family that has missed appointments, a letter may be in order. Not only is a letter a formal means of contacting the family, it is also an official record terminating therapy. In the letter, the therapist documents the length of contact and expresses specific concerns about the family or individual members. For example, if the therapist is concerned about suicidal tendencies of one of the members, this concern is spelled out. The letter concludes by inviting the family to recontact the therapist at any point.

Finally, although having families unexpectedly drop out of treatment is an occupational hazard, it behooves the therapist to identify any possible patterns in his or her caseload. For example, are many cases lost in the engagement phase? Do most dropouts occur in the middle phase of treatment? Are certain types of families more likely to drop out than others? Alcoholic families? Depressed families? Chaotic, acting-out families?

Consistent dropout patterns are feedback to observant therapists who are open to learning and improving their style. When such patterns are identified, constructive supervision serves as an invaluable aid for enhancing one's skill and benefiting the families with whom one works.

## *Summary*

Termination is more akin to closing a chapter than to closing a book. From a life cycle, developmental perspective, families do not reach an end point. They continually evolve from one generation to the next. The therapist enters a family to facilitate the unblocking of patterns that are inhibiting the family as a whole and the individual members from growing and then exits as soon as possible.

Certainly, the therapist's involvement—the creation of a therapeutic alliance—has a beginning, middle, and end, but it is an end for that specific time only. In fact, most family therapists' caseloads have their share of families that are being seen for the second or third time. This does not mean the first go-around in therapy was unsuccessful or incomplete. Rather, it indicates that the family members highly valued their first experience with the therapist—if they did not, they would find a new therapist—and are seeking assistance with another obstacle they have found difficult to hurdle.

From this longitudinal perspective, a therapist terminates with a family by consolidating the gains made in treatment, providing problem-solving skills for the future, and leaving the door open for additional contacts.

# *8*

# *Epilogue*

While teaching an introductory course in family counseling, I was approached by a student who said: "I'll be graduating with my master's in counseling in May and I'll then be opening a private practice in marital and family therapy. How do I go about the business of getting referrals?" Standing with my mouth open, I was undecided whether to burst out laughing or hit the student over the head. It struck me that after one introductory course in family counseling, the student barely knew the appropriate questions, much less the answers.

What struck me even more was his seemingly cavalier attitude toward working with people, particularly families. Working with people in the intimacy of therapy is a sacred trust, a responsibility one assumes in becoming a therapist. As a therapist, you will be looked upon as an "expert" by the people you work with, and your words will be weighed heavily. You are in a position to do a great deal of good or a great deal of harm. Consequently, you owe your clients the best that you can offer, and therefore you can never get enough experience, training, and supervision.

If you will permit me more soapbox statements, the following is a list of dos and don'ts regarding family therapy:

- Ask of family members only what you ask of yourself. Therapists can be notorious for asking clients to do the very behavior they themselves find difficult to do. For example, pushing a client to confront a spouse carries more authority if the therapist is also capable of such behavior.
- Similarly, don't rework your own family-of-origin issues with the families that come to you; do that in your own personal therapy.
- Likewise, don't attempt to remake families to fit an ideal goal. Ideal families exist in psychological theories and on television! Realistic treatment goals are much more likely to be reached than utopian heights.
- Let families teach and guide you. Each family has its own style, and understanding how each family functions expands your own knowledge base.

Your development as a family therapist and your professional reputation will spring from your ability to respect families and their individual members. This respect entails being direct and honest with the family members and doing your utmost to assist them with their difficulties. Research has shown that the effectiveness of any given therapy can vary considerably depending on what therapist is providing the treatment and that the major agent of effective psychotherapy is the therapist's personality (Luborsky, McLellan, Woody, O'Brien, & Auerbach, 1985). Consequently, your most valuable tool in developing your professional skill will not be techniques or theories but yourself.

# References

Alexander, J., & Parsons, B. (1982). *Functional family therapy.* Pacific Grove, CA: Brooks/Cole.

Anderson, C. M., & Stewart, S. (1983). *Mastering resistance: A practical guide to family therapy.* New York: Guilford Press.

Bandler, R., Grinder, J., & Satir, V. (1976). *Changing with families.* Palo Alto, CA: Science and Behavior Books.

Bergman, J. S. (1985). *Fishing for barracuda: Pragmatics of brief systemic therapy.* New York: Norton.

Bordin, E. S. (1982). A working alliance based model of supervision. *The Counseling Psychologist, 11:* 35–42.

Boss, P., & Greenberg, J. (1984). Family boundary ambiguity: A new variable in family stress theory. *Family Process, 23,* 535–546.

Boszormenyi-Nagy, I., & Spark, G. M. (1973). *Invisible loyalties: Reciprocity in intergenerational family therapy.* New York: Harper & Row.

Bowen, M. (1976). Theory in the practice of psychotherapy. In P. J. Guerin, Jr. (Ed.), *Family therapy: Theory and practice.* New York: Gardner Press.

Bowen, M. (1978). *Family therapy in clinical practice.* New York: Aronson.

Boyd-Franklin, N. (1987). The contribution of family therapy models to the treatment of black families. *Psychotherapy, 24(35),* 621–629.

Boyd-Franklin, N. (1989). *Black families in therapy: A multisystem approach.* New York: Guilford Press.

Byng-Hall, J., & Campbell, D. (1981). Resolving conflicts in family distance regulation: An integrative approach. *Journal of Marital and Family Therapy, 7(3),* 321–330.

Carter, E. (1988). Remarried families: Creating a new paradigm. In M. Walters, E. Carter, P. Papp, & O. Silverstein (Eds.), *The invisible web: Gender patterns in family relationships.* New York: Guilford Press.

Carter, E., & McGoldrick, M. (Eds.). (1988). *The changing family life cycle: A framework for family therapy* (2nd ed.). Boston: Allyn & Bacon.

Clingempeel, W. G., Grand, E., & Ievoli, R. (1984). Stepparent-stepchild relationships in stepmother and stepfather families: A multimethod study. *Family Relations, 33,* 465–473.

Combrinck-Graham, L. (1985). A developmental model for family systems. *Family Process, 24(2),* 139–150.

DeShazer, S. (1982). *Patterns of brief family therapy: An ecosystemic approach.* New York: Guilford Press.

Efran, J. S., Lukens, M. D., & Lukens, R. J. (1990). *Language, structure, and change: Frameworks of meaning in psychotherapy.* New York: Norton.

Falloon, I. R. (Ed.). (1986). *Handbook of behavioral family therapy.* New York: Guilford Press.

Frankl, V. E. (1975). Paradoxical intention and dereflection. *Psychotherapy Theory, Research and Practice, 12,* 226–237.

Glick, P. C., & Lin, Sung-Lin. (1986). Recent changes in divorce and remarriage. *Journal of Marriage and the Family, 48,* 737–747.

Goldenberg, I., & Goldenberg, H. (1991). *Family therapy: An overview* (3rd ed.). Pacific Grove, CA: Brooks/Cole.

Goolishian, H., & Anderson, H. (1987). Language systems and therapy: An evolving idea. *Psychotherapy, 24*(35), 529–538.

Goolishian, H., & Anderson, H. (1990). Understanding the therapeutic process: From individuals and families to systems language. In F. W. Kaslow (Ed.), *Voices in family psychology.* Newbury Park, CA: Sage.

Green, R., & Herget, M. (1991). Outcomes of systemic/strategic team consultation: III. The importance of therapist warmth and active structuring. *Family Process, 30,* 321–336.

Guerin, P. J., Jr., & Pendagast, M. A. (1976). Evaluation of family system and genogram. In P. J. Guerin, Jr. (Ed.), *Family therapy: Theory and practice.* New York: Gardner Press.

Gurman, A. S., & Kniskern, D. P. (1978). Deterioration in marital and family therapy: Empirical, clinical, and conceptual issues. *Family Process, 17,* 5.

Gurman, A. S., & Kniskern, D. P. (1991). *Handbook of family therapy: Vol. 2.* New York: Brunner/Mazel.

Gurman, A. S., Kniskern, D. P., & Pinsof, W. M. (1986). Research on the process and outcome of marital and family therapy. In S. L. Garfield & A. E. Bergin (Eds.), *Handbook of psychotherapy and behavior change.* New York: Wiley.

Haley, J. (1976). *Problem-solving therapy.* San Francisco: Jossey-Bass.

Hare-Mustin, R. T. (1989). The problems of gender in family therapy theory. In M. McGoldrick, C. M. Anderson, & F. Walsh (Eds.), *Women in families: A framework for family therapy.* New York: Norton.

Hoffman, L. (1981). *Foundations of family therapy: A conceptual framework for systems change.* New York: Basic Books.

Keeney, F. P., & Ross, J. M. (1985). *Mind in therapy: Constructing systemic family therapies.* New York: Basic Books.

Kerr, M., & Bowen, M. (1988). *Family evaluation.* New York: Norton.

Keshet, J. K., & Mirkin, M. P. (1985). Troubled adolescents in divorced and remarried families. In M. P. Mirkin & S. L. Koman (Eds.), *Handbook of adolescent and family therapy.* New York: Gardner Press.

L'Abate, L., Ganahl, G., & Hansen, J. C. (1986). *Methods of family therapy.* Englewood Cliffs, NJ: Prentice-Hall.

Liddle, H. A. (1983). Diagnosis and assessment in family therapy: A comparative analysis of six schools of thought. In J. C. Hansen & B. P. Keeney (Eds.), *Diagnosis and assessment in family therapy.* Rockville, MD: Aspen Systems.

Luborsky, L., McLellan, T., Woody, G. E., O'Brien, C. P., & Auerbach, A. (1985). Therapist success and its determinants. *Archives of General Psychiatry, 42,* 602–611.

Luepnitz, D. A. (1988). *The family interpreted: Feminist theory in clinical practice.* New York: Basic Books.

Lutz, P. (1983). The stepfamily: An adolescent perspective. *Family Relations, 32,* 367–375.

Mandanes, C. (1981). *Strategic family therapy.* San Francisco: Jossey-Bass.

Masters, R. S. (1978). Family therapy in child and adolescent psychiatry: A review of 35 families. *Child Psychiatry Quarterly, 11*(3), 70–82.

McGoldrick, M. (1982). Irish families. In M. McGoldrick, J. K. Pearce, & J. Giordano (Eds.), *Ethnicity and family therapy.* New York: Guilford Press.

McGoldrick, M., & Gerson, R. (1985). *Genograms in family assessment.* New York: Norton.

McGoldrick, M., Pearce, J. K., & Giordano, J. (1982). *Ethnicity and family therapy.* New York: Guilford Press.

Minuchin, S. (1974). *Families and family therapy.* Cambridge, MA: Harvard University Press.

Minuchin, S., & Fishman, H. C. (1981). *Family therapy techniques.* Cambridge, MA: Harvard University Press.

Mishne, J. M. (1986). *Clinical work with adolescents.* New York: Free Press.

Nelson, T. S., & Trepper, T. S. (1992). *101 Interventions in family therapy.* Binghamton, NY: Haworth Press.

Newberry, A. M., Alexander, J. F., & Turner, C. W. (1991). Gender as a process variable in family therapy. *Journal of Family Psychology, 5*(2), 158–175.

Nichols, M. P. (1987). *The self in the system: Expanding the limits of family therapy.* New York: Brunner/Mazel.

Nichols, M. P., & Schwartz, R. C. (1991). *Family therapy: Concepts and methods* (2nd ed.). Boston: Allyn & Bacon.

Orlinsky, D., & Howard, K. (1986). Process and outcome in psychotherapy. In S. L. Garfield & A. E. Bergin (Eds.), *Handbook of psychotherapy and behavior change.* New York: Wiley.

Papp, P. (1983). *The process of change.* New York: Guilford Press.

Piercy, F. P., & Sprenkle, D. H. (1986). *Family therapy sourcebook.* New York: Guilford Press.

Preto, N. G., & Travis, N. (1985). The adolescent phase of the family life cycle. In M. P. Mirkin & S. L. Koman (Eds.), *Handbook of adolescent and family therapy.* New York: Gardner Press.

Reiss, D. (1981). *The family's construction of reality.* Cambridge, MA: Harvard University Press.

Rotunno, M., & McGoldrick, M. (1982). Italian families. In M. McGoldrick, J. K. Pearce, & J. Giordano (Eds.), *Ethnicity and family therapy.* New York: Guilford Press.

Selvini Palazzoli, M. S., Cecchin, G., Boscolo, L., & Prata, G. (1978). *Paradox and counterparadox.* New York: Aronson.

Shapiro, R. (1981). Countertransference reactions in family therapy. In A. S. Gurman (Ed.), *Questions and answers in the practice of family therapy.* New York: Brunner/Mazel.

Sherman, R., & Fredman, N. (1986). *Handbook of structured techniques in marriage and family therapy.* New York: Brunner/Mazel.

Simon, R. M. (1988). Family life cycle issues in the therapy system. In B. Carter & M.

McGoldrick (Eds.), *The changing family life cycle* (2nd ed.). Boston: Allyn & Bacon.

Skynner, A. C. (1981). An open-systems, group-analytic approach to family therapy. In A. S. Gurman & D. P. Kniskern (Eds.), *Handbook of family therapy.* New York: Brunner/Mazel.

Spiegel, J. (1982). An ecological model of ethnic families. In M. McGoldrick, J. K. Pearce, & J. Giordano (Eds.), *Ethnicity and family therapy.* New York: Guilford Press.

Sprenkel, D. H., & Fisher, B. (1980). An empirical assessment of the goals of family therapy. *Journal of Marital and Family Therapy, 6,* 131–139.

Stanton, M. D., & Todd, T. C. (1979). Structural family therapy with drug addicts. In E. Kaufman & P. Kaufmann (Eds.), *The family therapy of drug and alcohol abuse.* New York: Gardner Press.

Steinglass, P., Bennett, L., Wolin, S., & Reiss, D. (1987). *The alcoholic family.* New York: Basic Books.

Titleman, P. (1987). *The therapist's own family: Toward the differentiation of self.* Northvale, NJ: Aronson.

Tomm, K. (1987a). Interventive interviewing: I. Strategizing as a fourth guideline for the therapist. *Family Process, 26,* 3–13.

Tomm, K. (1987b). Interventive interviewing: II. Reflexive questioning as a means to enable self-healing. *Family Process, 26,* 167–183.

Tomm, K. (1988). Interventive interviewing: III. Intending to ask lineal, circular, strategic, or reflexive questions? *Family Process, 27,* 1–15.

Visher, E., & Visher, J. (1988). *Old loyalties, new ties: Therapeutic strategies with stepfamilies.* New York: Brunner/Mazel.

Wallerstein, J. S., & Kelly, J. B. (1980). *Surviving the breakup: How children and parents cope with divorce.* New York: Basic Books.

Walsh, F., & Scheinkman, M. (1989). (Fe)male: The hidden gender dimension in models of family therapy. In M. McGoldrick, C. M. Anderson, & F. Walsh (Eds.), *Women in families: A framework for family therapy.* New York: Norton.

Walters, M., Carter, R., Papp, P., & Silverstein, O. (1988). *The invisible web: Gender patterns in family relationships.* New York: Guilford Press.

Watzlawick, P. (Ed.). (1984). *The invented reality: How do we know what we believe we know? Contributions to constructionism.* New York: Norton.

Watzlawick, P., Weakland, J., & Fisch, R. (1974). *Change: Principles of problem formation and problem resolution.* New York: Norton.

Whitaker, C. A., & Bumberry, W. M. (1988). *Dancing with the family: A symbolic-experiential approach.* New York: Brunner/Mazel.

Whitaker, C. A., & Keith, D. V. (1981). Symbolic-experiential family therapy. In A. S. Gurman & D. P. Kniskern (Eds.), *Handbook of family therapy.* New York: Brunner/Mazel.

Will, D. (1983). Some techniques for working with resistant families of adolescents. *Journal of Adolescence, 6*(1), 13–26.

Worden, M. (1991). *Adolescents and their families: An introduction to assessment and intervention.* Binghamton, NY: Haworth Press.

Wylie, M. S. (1991). Family therapy's neglected prophet. *The Family Therapy Networker, 15*(2), 24–46.

# Index

Boldface numbers in this index refer to the page on which the term is defined.

TO THE OWNER OF THIS BOOK:

We hope that you have found *Family Therapy Basics* useful. So that this book can be improved in a future edition, would you take the time to complete this sheet and return it? Thank you.

School and address: _____

Department: _____

Instructor's name: _____

1. What I like most about this book is: _____

_____

2. What I like least about this book is: _____

_____

3. My general reaction to this book is: _____

_____

4. The name of the course in which I used this book is: _____

_____

5. In the space below, or on a separate sheet of paper, please write specific suggestions for improving this book and anything else you'd care to share about your experience in using the book.

_____

_____

_____

_____

_____

_____

_____

_____

_____

Optional:

Your name: _____ Date: _____

May Brooks/Cole quote you either in promotion for *Family Therapy Basics* or in future publishing ventures?

Yes: _____ No: _____

Sincerely,

*Mark Worden*

Brooks/Cole is dedicated to publishing quality publications for education in the human services fields. If you are interested in learning more about our publications, please fill in your name and address and request our latest catalogue, using this prepaid mailer.

Name: _____

Street Address: _____

City, State, and Zip: _____

FOLD HERE

- - - - - - - - - - - - - - - - - - - - - - - - - - - - - - - - - - - -

BUSINESS REPLY MAIL

FIRST CLASS        PERMIT NO. 358        PACIFIC GROVE, CA

POSTAGE WILL BE PAID BY ADDRESSEE

ATT: _____ *Human Services Catalogue* _____

**Brooks/Cole Publishing Company**
**511 Forest Lodge Road**
**Pacific Grove, California  93950-9968**

- - - - - - - - - - - - - - - - - - - - - - - - - - - - - - - - - - - -

FOLD HERE